How to Choose a College Major

How to Choose a College Major

Revised and Updated Edition

LINDA LANDIS ANDREWS

McGraw-Hill

New York   Chicago   San Francisco   Lisbon   London
Madrid   Mexico City   Milan   New Delhi   San Juan
Seoul   Singapore   Sydney   Toronto

The McGraw·Hill Companies

1 2 3 4 5 6 7 8 9 10 FGR/FGR 0 9 8 7 6

ISBN 0-07-146784-X

 This book is printed on recycled, acid-free paper containing
a minimum of 50% recycled, de-inked fiber.

Library of Congress Cataloging-in-Publication Data

Andrews, Linda Landis.
    How to choose a college major / by Linda Landis Andrews.—Rev. and
updated ed.
        p. cm.
    ISBN 0-07-146784-X (alk. paper)
    1. College majors--United States.   I. Title.
    LB2361.5.A45 2006
    378.1'9422—dc22

                                                    2005023702

For you, the student beginning on your exciting journey
May you always remember
"Industria ditat." (Hard work pays.)

Contents

Preface   xiii

Acknowledgments   xv

CHAPTER 1   **A Major Decision**   1

AN IMPORTANT DECISION—YEARS AND DOLLARS SAVED
CALCULATE BEFORE YOU LEAP
A WORLD-CLASS PROBLEM SOLVER
PROBLEM-SOLVING STYLES—A TRIP TO THE VIDEO STORE
WHAT A MAJOR MEANS TODAY
TECHNOLOGY CHANGES MAJORS
TECHNOLOGY CHANGES ACCESS
NEW MAJORS HAVE BEEN ADDED
KEEPING UP WITH THE COMPETITION
THE SHRINKING WORLD
MULTICULTURALISM
POPULARITY OF MAJORS
THE CONNECTION BETWEEN MAJORS AND CAREERS
WHEN TO DECLARE A MAJOR?
EARLY DECISION MAKERS
HOW DO I DECLARE A MAJOR?
THE REALITIES OF COLLEGE TODAY
SUCCESS MEANS JUMPING THROUGH MANY HOOPS:
    BUREAUCRACY AND FORMS
REGISTRATION
GETTING THE BEST INSTRUCTORS
PREREQUISITES
LIFE INTRUSIONS
SHOULDERING THE COST
PERSONAL SUCCESS TOOLS
WEIGHING THE PROS AND CONS

DO YOU HAVE THE STAMINA?
SUCCESSFUL TACTICS FOR STAYING ON COURSE
FORGET WHAT THEY TOLD YOU IN PRESCHOOL:
    TALK TO STRANGERS
FORCES THAT SWAY MAJOR DECISIONS
GUIDES TO THE TERRITORY
DEVELOP PATIENCE
TIPS FOR FINDING THE RIGHT MAJOR FOR YOU
THE PRIZE IS WORTH THE EFFORT

CHAPTER 2   **Who Am I? Time to Take Stock**   **23**

MANY TOOLS ARE AVAILABLE TO YOU
WRITING AS SELF-DISCOVERY
SKILLS YOU HAVE NOW
VALUES
THE THREE PARTS AS TRIPOD
THE TOTAL PICTURE

CHAPTER 3   **Guiding Lights**   **39**

SEARCHLIGHTS: HIGH SCHOOL GUIDANCE COUNSELORS
BE A DETECTIVE
LOOKING AT THE WIDE FIELD OF CHOICES
STARLIGHTS: YOUR HUNCHES AND DREAMS
THE PARENT FACTOR
TIME-OUT
ENLIGHTENMENT: CAREER DAYS AND NIGHTS
BEACONS: INFORMATION INTERVIEWS
TESTING
INDEPENDENT EDUCATIONAL CONSULTANTS

CHAPTER 4   **Tasks to Jump-Start Your Search**   **59**

A WORKING CALENDAR FOR HIGH SCHOOL STUDENTS
A WORKING CALENDAR FOR COLLEGE STUDENTS

OTHER MISSIONS TO ACCOMPLISH
DOING YOUR HOMEWORK ON MAJORS
YOUR PART-TIME JOB

CHAPTER 5   **Descriptions of Majors**   75

ANTHROPOLOGY
ART
ART THERAPY
BIOLOGY
BUSINESS ADMINISTRATION
CHEMISTRY
CLASSICS
COMMUNICATION AND THEATRE
COMPUTER SCIENCE
CRIMINAL JUSTICE
ECONOMICS
EDUCATION
ENGINEERING
ENGLISH
ENVIRONMENTAL SCIENCES
FRENCH
GEOGRAPHY
GEOLOGY
KINESIOLOGY
MATHEMATICS
MEDICAL TECHNOLOGY
MUSIC
NURSING
OCCUPATIONAL THERAPY
PHILOSOPHY
PHYSICS
POLITICAL SCIENCE
PSYCHOLOGY
RELIGIOUS STUDIES
SOCIAL WORK
SOCIOLOGY

THEATRE
KEEP ON SEARCHING

CHAPTER 6   **Courses for Different Majors**   **97**

GRINDERS, WEEDERS, BREEZES
PREREQUISITES
THE MAJORS

CHAPTER 7   **New, Unusual, and
Design-Your-Own Majors**   **117**

TOY DESIGN
MULTILINGUAL JOURNALISM
HUMAN ECOLOGY
LEADERSHIP STUDIES
THERAPEUTIC RIDING
PEACE STUDIES
CULTURE, BRAIN, AND DEVELOPMENT
EMERGENCY ADMINISTRATION AND PLANNING
SYNOPTIC MAJORS
TURFGRASS MANAGEMENT
AERONAUTICAL SCIENCE
BACHELOR OF ARTS IN ENGINEERING
RESIDENTIAL PROPERTY MANAGEMENT
HAWAIIAN STUDIES
SPORT SCIENCES
BAGPIPING
ELECTRONIC MEDIA, ARTS, AND COMMUNICATION
VISUAL EFFECTS AND MOTION GRAPHICS
INTERNATIONAL THEATER PRODUCTION
INTERACTIVE MEDIA AND GAME DEVELOPMENT
INTERCULTURAL STUDIES FOR BUSINESS
HEALTH COMMUNICATIONS
ADVENTURE RECREATION

LESBIAN, GAY, AND BISEXUAL STUDIES
EQUESTRIAN BUSINESS MANAGEMENT
RANCH MANAGEMENT
FISHERIES
DESIGN YOUR OWN MAJOR

CHAPTER 8 **Choose a Major, Then Concentrate on Skills** **139**

PRESENTATION SKILLS
LISTENING SKILLS
COMMUNICATION SKILLS
WRITING SKILLS
PHONE SKILLS
E-MAIL SKILLS
CRITICAL-THINKING SKILLS
INTERPERSONAL SKILLS
ORGANIZATIONAL SKILLS
RESEARCH SKILLS
A PROFESSIONAL VOCABULARY
CONCENTRATION
COACHABILITY
CREATIVITY
TECHNOLOGICAL SKILLS
PLANNING SKILLS
ACCOUNTABILITY
PERCEPTIVITY
TOLERANCE
COPING SKILLS
INITIATIVE AND LEADERSHIP SKILLS
PERSEVERANCE

CHAPTER 9 **Learning from Others: Real People Talk about Their Majors** **155**

CHAPTER 10   **Jobs for the Twenty-First Century 179**

WHO KNOWS BETTER THAN UNCLE SAM?
LOOK IN YOUR OWN BACKYARD
THE GOVERNMENT'S CRYSTAL BALL
INTERESTING FACTS
SPECIFIC JOB INFORMATION

CHAPTER 11   **Famous People and Their Majors 191**

APPENDIX   **National Associations 197**

Preface

Understanding that you have more choices than you thought possible is the beginning of wisdom. And freedom. The poet was wrong about the road less traveled. To travel down one road does not mean excluding the others. You still have to carry the same backpack.

Some people will tell you that college is "the time of your life." They envy your youth, your energy, your choices. They have forgotten how burdensome these can be without a compass.

Imagine your choices, cast your net far and wide, celebrate your decisions, and, as I tell my daughter every time she approaches a new journey, "Remember, your job is to have fun."

Acknowledgments

Thanks to the graduates of many schools who shared their personal stories of how they chose a major and the outcomes in their professional lives. Appreciation also is due to Jana Wichelecki and Thomas Stearns for their many hours of research. I'm grateful for the patience of my family, Clark, Bree, and Patrick, who listened attentively the many times I talked about the progress of this book. The cheerful encouragement of Monica Bentley at McGraw-Hill made the task easier. Thanks to all of you for being on the same page with me.

How to Choose
a College Major

A MAJOR DECISION

"What's your major?"

This question bounces around campus, in the cafeteria, at basketball games, in movie lines, causing anxiety in the hearts and minds of undergraduates. This nagging question plays like a loud, incessant drumbeat over the quadrangle. Students who are supremely confident have surefire, too-quick answers, but others are more tentative:

"I was a nursing major but now I'm in kinesiology."

"I don't know, I'm still deciding."

"My father thinks I should be in engineering, but I'm more interested in history."

"I'm switching to poli sci. I'm tired of making myself miserable with business courses I'm not interested in."

How can anyone be certain at age 18 about the question of a major? Some students have a Velcro-like focus and stick to their choice all the way through college. But, for many students, choosing a major is a difficult and sometimes agonizing decision.

Many students, and you may be one of them, lack information in four areas:

1. Personal information about yourself: interests, aptitude, motivation, and values
2. Knowledge of what particular majors mean
3. Information on how majors interact with careers
4. Skills needed after graduation

This information is available, but it takes time to gather. This book will help you to find all the information you need to make an intelligent decision. When you are finished gathering the information, you will choose a major based on insight, not guesswork.

An Important Decision—Years and Dollars Saved

Why do students spend an average of six years in college today?

Many are working and going to school at the same time. But an overwhelming factor is the number of students changing majors in midstream. Millions of dollars are spent each year in the United States on majors that students change before graduation day. Declaring a major without sufficient preparation often leads to worry, frustration, loss of sleep, discouragement, and a feeling of having to start all over again. The saying is shopworn but apt: Look before you leap.

The cost of this confusion continues to rise as college costs escalate. The price tag at some elite private schools exceeds $40,000 per student, per year. Tuition and expenses for in-state residents at some first-tier public universities have passed $10,000 yearly. By the time you read this book, costs may have climbed even higher. If you find this book in 2040 on the dusty back shelf of a library, know that the tuition you're paying now will seem quaint in the future also.

Calculate before You Leap

According to the FinAid! (www.fafsa.org) Web site, on average, tuition tends to increase by about 8 percent per year. An 8 percent college inflation rate means that the cost of college doubles every nine years. For a baby born today, this means that college costs will be more than three times the current rates when the child enters college. At a school that costs $42,000 today, this means that the costs will rise to $84,000 in 2015.

And, even if money is not a concern, parents worry about the possibility of spending that money and their child having no meaningful job upon graduation. Add to this a year or more of taking courses in a wrong major and the costs go up. This is an enormous waste of time and energy and can be avoided.

By reading this book and following the suggestions in it, you will save yourself much unneeded confusion and countless dollars. College is a time to meet new people, explore ideas, and grow as a person. This period should not be spoiled by needless anxiety about your major. Information is power and is within your grasp. Be patient with yourself on this journey of discovery, and you'll win the rewards.

A World-Class Problem Solver

Executives say they are looking for people who can solve problems. Choosing a major will build your problem-solving skills. Your number 1 goal now is to solve the problem of choosing a major. This challenge can serve as a blueprint for other important decisions in the years ahead. And you'll be able to add "good problem solver" to your résumé.

Problem-Solving Styles—A Trip to the Video Store

Think about what happens when you take a trip to the video store with your friends. When you get there, titles scream out from categories such as foreign films, new releases, dramas, horror, poker videos. You strain to remember what you've heard about the different films. Much of your impressions will come from advertising you've seen, word of mouth, and reviews. Most people go into the video store with an open mind, hoping for inspiration. They browse, see what's available, read the film jackets, ask attractive strangers what they think, and finally make a decision.

Is there a correlation between choosing a major and choosing a rental movie? How can these two activities be the same? Consider the process of confusion, investigation, and conclusion. You're confused about a major, you ask people about subjects, and you reach a decision. And one of the tenets of good problem solving is to remember that few decisions are irrevocable. If you don't like the movie you rented, you turn off the DVD player and vow never to rent another film starring Ben Affleck. If you choose a major and the first few courses are disappointing, you can reconsider. Don't give up your first choice of major, however, unless you have talked to your professors during office hours about your choice of major. Professors are lonely people during office hours; they want students to visit.

What a Major Means Today

A *major* means taking approximately 32 class hours in a specific subject area, such as music. A list of typical majors and their descriptions is provided in Chapter 5. Chapter 6 contains a list of courses typically required in some majors. A course may carry any number of credit hours, but most courses carry three or four credits hours. Each major has a certain number of required courses and electives, which you choose on your own within the field. These give you freedom to follow your interests. A theater major, for instance, might take improvisation as an elective, besides the required courses such as stage design, acting, and history of theater.

A *minor* is your secondary field of interest and requires fewer courses. Double majors have become popular as students seek the best competitive advantage in anticipation of entering the world of work, for instance, double majoring in business and communications. Many colleges have loosened the barriers between subjects and allow students greater freedom to choose from different categories of courses in defining interdisciplinary majors, such as taking classes in philosophy and anthropology.

Technology Changes Majors

Today's major isn't what it used to be even 10 years ago. Technology has revolutionized research that you'll be doing in your major, making information on any subject more accessible and broader in scope. Computers allow students to research further and faster than ever before.

The field of library science, for instance, has been revolutionized by technology. In the old days, students found information organized through Melvil Dewey's decimal system. They pulled out wooden drawers filled with cards giving the names of authors, books, and codes indicating where the books could be found on shelves. Today, students hit keys and use search engines such as IX Quick, Lycos, Excite, or Google for their research. Librarians have become cyberspace experts, guiding students through the maze of electronic information.

The revolution has not happened the way it had been predicted, however. Not long ago people were predicting that by the year 2000 libraries would be gone, replaced by digital sources of information. Today colleges have revamped their libraries into information commons with clusters of computers, coffee shops, comfortable chairs, and 24-hour technical help.

Similarly, technology has revolutionized the world of graphic artists, who are now trained to move easily between print and electronic design, text and illustration, and photo and illustration. The computer has enhanced creativity, allowing artists to cross boundaries between media. Graphic artists no longer rely solely on their inner creativity and intuition. Technology has advanced their field with new programs, new ways to create. In a very fundamental way, their creativity has been changed by technology.

Your major will continue to change. *Parade* magazine (June 5, 2005) predicted, "Many of today's kids will work at jobs not yet invented." The magazine asks, "How many farmers in 1899 would have thought the U.S. would need 139,000 psychologists a century later?" So, don't fret; it's all going to evolve into something else anyway.

Technology Changes Access

Students are required to learn the computer skills they will need to complete research in their major. Certain computer labs are equipped with specialized software for specific majors, such as accounting. Futurists are predicting that degrees will be earned on the Internet through a combination of courses at different colleges. In this future scenario, students hypothetically might be able to take a course at a school in Minnesota, one from Boston, and the rest from their original campus, all via the Internet.

New Majors Have Been Added

And many new majors have been added. Thirty years ago few colleges offered a major in women's studies; today most offer at least a minor in women's studies. As the culture changes, students are interested in new subjects. Professors, intrigued with researching a new area, suggest a new course. More research is conducted, and a few more courses are added. The evolution is completed when the subject area is offered as a major. In Chapter 7, you will see descriptions of majors, such as toy design and international theater production, that have been created as interest in these subjects has evolved.

Keeping Up with the Competition

Today approximately 12 percent of the U.S. population (295.7 million people) holds a degree from a four-year college. Despite this low percentage, some people think that today's college degree holds the prestige that a high school degree did in your grandparents' day. To stay ahead of the pack, some students immediately start graduate school after college graduation. Others enroll in graduate school because they find their job options limited after college. For these reasons, your choice of major is not as important as it was in years past. However, certain jobs will require that you continue on to earn a master's degree. When you choose a major, consider also whether you will need an advanced degree to succeed in your field.

The Shrinking World

The rise of markets in the Far East, Latin America, and Europe has increased competition for jobs, even for college-educated people. For example, a U.S. firm in South America recruited a U.S. college graduate to help establish a chain of movie theaters. He was sent to London for training in the movie theater management business and then worked in Chile managing multiplex movie houses. A big-city mayor hired a team of college graduates to develop trade relations with Central America. Highly skilled in presentations, the team traveled and worked 60-hour weeks promoting trade for the city.

Building business abroad has become a major challenge to the American economy. Increasingly, many American companies want their employees to have experience working abroad so that they are comfortable in emerging markets. But this has a downside for graduates looking for work. In seeking jobs with U.S. firms, U.S. college graduates find themselves in competition with people from other countries.

Multiculturalism

Multiculturalism, understanding and appreciating reality in different cultures, has affected many majors. Also affecting majors has been a distrust of relying on the information provided solely by "dead white men." There has been a push to discover and appreciate the work of all people of different hues from different continents and to celebrate the differences.

Popularity of Majors

As majors change in popularity, there may be fewer opportunities to pursue a "hot" major; so many students are after the "prize" that becomes more elusive. "Health-related majors remain as the top choice of major for college-bound Seniors," said Ellen Sawtell, the College Board's Associate Director of Data & Reporting in 2005. "Business and social science/history also continue to rank high as the second and third choices. These choices have consistently been the top three for the past ten years," she added. If you are interested in pursuing any of these popular fields, plan to compete for admissions and classes. Knowledge of deadlines and restrictions will help you in beating the pack.

The Connection between Majors and Careers

Majors and careers are tightly tied together today. Parents want to know what their offspring is going to "do" after graduation. Thirty years ago people went to college to learn how to think, to gain an educated perspective. They learned theory and relied on an employer after college to teach them the specifics of how to earn a living. There were notable exceptions: engineering, speech therapy, and nursing. The emphasis, however, was on becoming educated. Most people who went to college received a broad education, learning about such subjects as existentialism, the Supreme Court, and workers' rights. Today much more of the responsibility of training people falls on colleges and universities. As the cost of education has accelerated, so has the expectation of return on the dollar.

As a result of this new focus, interaction with the outside world is crucial. Many working professionals teach a class, bringing their special expertise to campus. Students are encouraged to take multiple internships or cooperative education jobs before they reach the job market so that they will have a realistic view of what they will be doing. The world is moving too quickly to delay awareness until graduation.

When to Declare a Major

At most schools majors are declared in spring of sophomore year. Here's a typical schedule:

Freshman and Sophomore Year

1. Take a variety of classes.
2. Talk to professors.
3. Compare ideas about majors with upperclass students.
4. Visit the career counseling office.
5. Attend seminars on majors and career paths.
6. Talk to working professionals about their majors in college.
7. Think about a double major or a minor that complements your major.

In the spring of your sophomore year, you will face the "major" decision, probably second-guessing yourself a few times. You still have time. In the first semester of your junior year courses in the major will help you determine if your declared major will hold your interest.

Early Decision Makers

A few students know what interests them from an early age. Ed Cook was raised near Boston, the land of early American history and the Pilgrims, Paul Revere's ride, Lexington and Concord. "History was something I clearly liked in junior high, and it was always the thing that fascinated me in high school. It was a natural progression to a major in college," says Cook. For his senior paper at Harvard he researched the early eighteenth century social history of a New England town, Dedham, Massachusetts. The town had well-preserved minutes of town meetings and tax lists. A particularly strong historical society had collected papers and diaries, for which he was grateful. Cook earned his doctorate in early American history at Johns Hopkins University and now teaches at the University of Chicago. He has written a book, *The Fathers of the Towns, Leadership and Community Development in 18th Century New England*. His career interest started in junior high and never wavered.

Most students need more time, realizing that they can't possibly know what each major entails, what they're good at, or how the workplace is viewing a particular major today. It may surprise you to know that some people don't discover a subject they feel passionate about until they are age 40 or older. Trying to know your life's work at 18 is asking a great deal of yourself.

How Do I Declare a Major?

Your college catalog will indicate the specific way that you declare a major. Usually it involves contacting the department in which the major is taught and formally declaring the major in writing. Some departments require an application and a certain grade point average.

After you declare a major, you will probably be assigned an adviser in the department. At large schools students frequently reach graduation without ever seeing an adviser. This is unfortunate because advisers can be very helpful. How?

1. By reminding you to take all the required courses
2. By certifying the transferability of summer school credit from another college
3. By providing all the information needed to graduate

The Realities of College Today

More than 17 million students are attending college today and trying to make the right choice about their major. Some will graduate not knowing what they can do with their major. Others, like you, will have done the necessary homework to find:

1. What interests you
2. What your talents are
3. What your values are
4. How to match these with a career

The goal is to choose a major wisely and not spend unnecessary extra time and money in college.

Success Means Jumping through Many Hoops: Bureaucracy and Forms

If you let it, the bureaucracy of colleges and universities will eat you alive. All the forms you must fill out, the deadlines you must meet, and the people you must talk to about your particular situation, can destroy brain cells. Not really. After a while, however, these daily challenges become part of life. As a student facing them for the first time, you may be overwhelmed. As you learn shortcuts for getting through the red tape, the process will become second nature. Tackling the bureaucracy is definitely a college skill that will help you succeed on the outside.

Remedy One. People skills are what will guide you through the college bureaucracy. These skills do not come automatically. You have to learn how to talk to clerical staff, teaching assistants, lecturers, financial aid personnel, counselors, and professors. If you are too shy to ask for permission to join a class that you need, now is the time to get past it. Start by asking people for things you don't care about. During the day you might ask five people for the time. With nothing at stake, you can try different approaches. Are people more apt to help you when you are bold? polite? indifferent? menacing? Find what works for you.

Remedy Two. Pay attention to detail. If you remember to dot every i, cross every t, and keep copies of everything, you will be way ahead of the game. When you talk to people on the phone, be sure to write down the date and the name of the person who gave you information.

Speaking of keeping copies, be sure to keep either hard copies of papers you submit in class or copies on disks. Too often papers get lost. Even professors lose grade records online. Years after you complete a course, you may need a hard or disk copy of a research paper for different reasons: for example, to refresh the memory of a professor writing a letter of recommendation for you or to show work you have researched to a prospective employer.

Remedy Three. Be sure to maintain a sense of humor. If you can laugh at the stupid things that happen to you, you will be less likely to implode. Laughing will help you keep things in perspective.

Remember the rule of replacement: The crisis in your life today will be replaced by another crisis six months in the future.

Registration

Majors have been lost and won on the basis of what was available at the time of registration. Usually upperclass students, members of clubs, the honors society, the mayor's nephew, and athletes have first choice. If you can't get into the prerequisites for your major or can't fill your schedule with the requisites for your major, it begins to feel futile. As with the other many lessons students learn in college, motivation is the key. Find out how you can get advanced priority for registration. So, you have to join a club. When you can't get into a class, talk to the professor. E-mail her. Beg. You are not going to be a math major if you cannot get into Calculus I.

Getting the Best Instructors

On campus tours parents frequently ask how many classes are taught by professors versus how many are taught by teaching assistants (TAs). The parents imagine that if more teaching is done by professors, then their child will receive a better education. Not necessarily. Professors frequently are preoccupied with their research. Teaching assistants bring energy and newness to the job and might be more accessible than professors.

Whether it's a professor or a teaching assistant, getting the good ones for all your classes is the challenge. What does "good" mean? Generally it means relating to students and being able to communicate with them. It means being fair in assignments and grading. It means being up-to-date in the field. Being taught well can make the difference between a grade of A and D. Or it can make the difference between your being excited about your major or discouraged.

Shop Around. Look at Pick-a-Prof.com to see if your school is registered. At some schools the student government publishes an online guide to the instructors with data gathered from students. Questionnaires ask students whether the instructor grades fairly and about the workload, instructor's presentation style, and availability during office hours. And they encourage students to write additional comments.

Check Your Progress. Don't blindly sign up for a course without trying to find out about the instructor. Ask questions of upperclass students. See if the syllabus, the instructor's plan for the course, is online before the term begins. Usually the syllabus includes the instructor's policies regarding grading, plagiarism, and attendance and what is expected of students who take the course. Some syllabi include cartoons or ridiculous statements, which are included to make sure you are reading it. The syllabi of others are formal. What most students care about is substance, fairness in grading, and a clear sense of what is going on in the course.

Prerequisites

Most freshmen take introductory courses unless they have tested out of the required courses. Typically, this happens when a student has had a great deal of advanced preparation in high school, say four years of French and living with a French family for a term. Predictably, this person is much more likely to score highly and place out of French 101 than someone who doesn't know what a croissant is. So, freshman year can be a treading-water year while you investigate where each major leads.

Many times students get discouraged in their freshman year—the sections might be large, students are talking on their cell phones during the lecture, and the class feels like a huge sea of confusion and doesn't generate any real excitement about learning a new subject. Pay your dues—you have to take these lower-level courses as prerequisites for the upper-level, more intense courses that provide the excitement of a major.

Life Intrusions

Even the best-laid plans sometimes go haywire. You register for the course you need, you start the course, and you just don't grasp the material. You go to the tutors on campus and you visit the professor during office hours, but nothing works. Almost everyone in college has had this experience. You may not be ready for this course yet. Perhaps next term the material will be easier to grasp. Drop the course.

The agony of dealing with such a situation isn't worth it. Summer school is tough because a whole term of material is condensed, for instance, 16 weeks to 8 weeks. But staying in the course may discourage you too much from pursuing the major you have chosen.

It's also possible that a semester is especially tough because of personal problems you're wrestling with. Students struggle to form and maintain new relationships, which brings tremendous stress. The parents of college-age students may provide worries for students: a serious health problem, loss of job, divorce, relocation for a new job. Consider how much outside stress you are under before you change majors. Your original major choice may be entirely appropriate, but the course you are taking during a time of stress may discourage you.

Shouldering the Cost

The high cost of college is a fact of life. Students used to be resigned to college costs, thinking they would be compensated with higher-paying jobs. Now, they are not certain a job slot awaits them at the end of the graduation line. A freshman at Northwestern University interviewed on the *Today Show* said he became nervous every time he took a test or handed in a paper, knowing how much his education was costing and feeling the pressure. The pressure is pervasive. Students feel they must choose a major that will ensure them of the ability to pay off their student loans. They feel pressured knowing how privileged they are to even be attending such an expensive school.

Remedy One. Remember that time is on your side. You may have a great deal of debt, but you are young. You will have 40 years of productive work life to pay off student loans.

Remedy Two. Realize that your education will not end in school. In any career you have the option of adding skills that will benefit you through your paycheck. You will have the option of taking on new responsibilities to add to your own prosperity.

Remedy Three. Remember that the cost of education will grow. So you are taking advantage of the lowest possible price.

Personal Success Tools

You can't accomplish any task without the help of a set of personal success tools. You'll need the following to succeed:

Decision Making

Learning how to make the best decisions for yourself is a skill that will be helpful the rest of your days. You already have started making good decisions. Here's the evidence:

- You have identified the challenge—searching for the best major for you.
- You have started to gather information by reading this book and talking to others.
- You have not panicked and picked the first option that seemed feasible.

Becoming aware of how you have made decisions in the past is helpful. You have seen classmates and friends in different types of ineffective decision-making modes, such as:

- Accepting the first idea that presents itself
- Being easily persuaded by others
- Seeing no clear correlation between decisions and goals
- Relying on faulty information

Obviously, you will be the opposite. You will:

- Investigate several ideas before making a decision.
- Be independent in your thinking and not be easily swayed by others.
- Have a clear idea of goals and how decisions affect them.
- Check and recheck information to be sure it is accurate.

Gathering Information

Research is one of the main tasks students perform at college. They comb databases. They collect useful Web sites on their computers. They investigate in the laboratory. They gather wisdom from faculty members. Students are trained not to jump to early conclusions. Particularly in the case of choosing a major, you cannot skip the information-gathering stage. Lack of information creates indecisiveness. Weighing the pros and cons of each interesting major is impossible if you don't have enough information to put on each side of the scale. Consider the following example.

> Two freshmen are making out their sophomore year schedules at a large university. One, Bradford, has just pledged a fraternity and takes the advice of a junior in the fraternity house about what courses to take. The other, Isaac, talks to an adviser in his college about the distribution of credits required for graduation, studies the college catalog to make sure he understands the course sequence, and then double-checks with the college advising office to make sure that what he needs is being offered the following year. Isaac invests time and energy into getting the information. Isaac also gets a signed note from the adviser so that later he will have proof of what he was told and by whom. Isaac's funny that way. Whenever he gets information of any kind over the phone or in person, he asks for the name of the person he's speaking with. And he keeps his notes. On the other hand, Bradford may luck out, but who wants to rely on luck?

Rules and requirements change regularly. You can receive five different pieces of information from five people in the same division of a college. Three of those people may have been hired last week.

Majors change also. Industries are quite fickle in what they want from college graduates. If you at least investigate beforehand what you are going to major in, the surprise of a new trend won't be as great.

Collecting Viewpoints

Imagine all the different personalities on a collection of baseball cards. When talking to people about majors, remember that everyone has a different basis for his or her opinion. Some people think a major is desirable only if it leads to your making a lot of money. Others hold a very traditional view of what college should be. In the traditional view of college students read, research, and study subjects that have no direct connection to a job description.

Parents sometimes are biased for or against what they majored in. Or they may feel that college isn't necessary because they didn't go. People have a bias based on their own experiences. Gathering many opinions will give you wisdom about a particular major. Just as in any range, the opinions at each end will be the extremes, and the truth will lie somewhere in the middle.

The exciting part of your investigation is the learning curve. When you start out, you will know very little, but bit by bit each piece of information will add to your heap until you will have amassed a great deal of knowledge.

Some of the information will be contradictory. Perhaps an impression is out of date or not based on a wide enough sample. When two opinions conflict, choose the opinion of the person who seems more reliable. And be careful of people spouting offhand opinions that sound like the truth but aren't. For example, someone says to you, "There are no jobs for English majors." This is completely false. In Chapter 9, "Learning from Others," students will tell you why.

Weighing the Pros and Cons

If you've gathered your information but are still unclear about what to do, it's time to weigh the pros and cons. Draw a line down the middle of a piece of paper and write the words "Pros" in one column and "Cons" in the other. This approach enables analysis of the situation and promotes thinking in a different way. Typical column items might include:

Number of years in school required for this major
Difficulty of courses
Natural ability
Enjoyment of the subject
Motivation to study this subject
Value you put on this subject
Jobs available after graduation
Salary ranges
Cost of earning this degree

Moira's Story. Here's the chart of Moira, a student weighing the pros and cons of majoring in physical therapy:

PROS	CONS
Natural aptitude	Number of years in school required for this major
Motivated to study this subject	Difficulty of courses (not sure she can earn good grades)
Enjoys the subject	Does not know anyone in the field
Jobs available after graduation	
Good pay	
Considers this subject worthwhile and valuable	

Through research, Moira has learned that she will eventually need a master's degree and that getting accepted into a program is difficult. As far as the difficulty of the courses is concerned, she needs to take prep courses before declaring her major. Many students cannot earn good grades in the large science sections. She must evaluate whether being a physical therapist means enough to her to struggle for the good grades. She needs a plan of action to be successful, leaving as little as possible to chance. Talking to recent graduates in physical therapy will be helpful in assessing whether her interest in helping people who have had strokes or other physical problems will be sufficient motivation for her to put in the hard work required in the courses for the major.

She finds a physical therapist through her pharmacist uncle and spends a morning watching her interact with patients. She is impressed with how much the patients rely on the physical therapist to teach them how to rebuild their lives.

After talking with people on campus, Moira realizes that every major is difficult and that physical therapy courses are probably no tougher than other disciplines. She decides to go for it.

Postscript: Today Moira has a master's degree in physical therapy and works in the professional offices of a suburban hospital.

Sean's Story. Sean comes from a family of cops. His father and uncles have told him that if he wants to go into law enforcement in the future, his options will be better with a college degree in criminal justice.

Following is Sean's chart, on the pros and cons of majoring in criminal justice:

PROS	CONS
Motivated to study this subject	Strong competition for jobs
Courses not too difficult	Lower salary
Enjoys the subject	Tied too closely to family expectations
Natural aptitude	
Family in law enforcement	
Police scholarship available	
Fits with his values	

Although Sean is confident that he can get through the program, he is not sure there will be a job for him when he finishes. Also, he feels as if he's considering this field because it is the only one he knows, through his family.

Postscript. Sean decided he did not have enough information to make a decision. He talked with a career counselor and several police officers who were not related to him. Still unsure, he decided to get training as an emergency medical technician (EMT), which involves 120 class hours plus 10 hours of internship in a hospital emergency room. He believes this will give him added exposure to police work in order to determine if he wants to major in criminal justice. Plus, he thinks it will be exciting.

Creating Your Chart

Your chart of pros and cons will be extremely helpful to you in weighing your choices. Fill in as many benefits and negatives as you can. If you don't know the pros and cons, now is the time to find out. Make a chart for each major you are considering.

MAJOR:

PROS	CONS
_____	_____
_____	_____
_____	_____
_____	_____
_____	_____
_____	_____

Do You Have the Stamina?

You need to consider whether you have enough interest in the major to plow through some uninteresting courses along with the exciting ones. Not all the courses will be enticing, but most will be interesting if you have made the right choice of a major. (Chapter 6 reviews courses typical for each major.)

Successful Tactics for Staying on Course

Surviving in school and getting through the prerequisites require that you do the following:

- Be patient with yourself.
- Realize that there is no perfect way to get through college. The journey has its ups and downs like any other life journey.
- Expect setbacks: a killer course, a broken ankle, a computer failure that wipes out a paper the night before it's due.
- Develop your people and negotiating skills.
- Keep hard or disk copies of every paper you submit.
- Develop contacts in class whom you can call with questions about the material.
- Seek help for personal problems through the school's counseling center.
- Ask for help. Much more help is available on campuses than students use.
- Vary your tasks every day.
- Make room for a social life. Spending your days in the company solely of books or your computer is too one-dimensional a way to live and is not good for your mental or physical health.

Forget What They Told You in Preschool: Talk to Strangers

Your willingness to strike up conversations with strangers will ensure you of an interesting social life at college. Hillary Clinton has said that she walked up to Bill Clinton in the Yale law library and said, "If you're going to keep looking at me and I'm going to keep looking back, we might as well be introduced. I'm Hillary Rodham." All your life, people have been telling you not to talk to strangers, but in college many old ideas have to be discarded. A wealth of interesting people exists on every campus. A painless way to meet such people is by joining a club or other interest group on campus or in the nearby community.

The first few weeks on campus may be daunting, especially with the swirl of unfamiliar classrooms, faces, and faculty members greeting you. College administrators, hoping to retain the students, offer orientation programs to help students make the transition from high school to college. Frequently, freshmen come to campus before school starts to meet new people and attend seminars on cultural diversity, date rape, alcohol awareness, and other social issues. With new freedom, students must make choices about how to manage their time and money, whom to socialize with, and how to succeed in a new environment.

Experiment, take chances, and get out of your room and dorm. Be sure you explore all the facilities on campus and activities that are available to you. Getting comfortable is a major task.

Forces That Sway Major Decisions

Old ideas about what a major means, or stereotypes, often influence students' decisions about majors. Accounting is a good example. In the past, accountants were considered number crunchers who had no personality and ate at their desks. Now, interaction with clients is considered highly important in the field of accounting, and students majoring in this field must have good people skills. Also, many accountants find that a great deal of time is spent selling their expertise to gain new clients, especially companies. Students who choose accounting today must have developed their oral and written communication skills and their ability to be comfortable with people.

Every major has changed in the past 20 years because of changing forces in society. Parents and students talk with astonishment about what they find out about majors after visiting several schools. And once people graduate, they must still keep up to date in their field through additional courses and seminars, or they will fall behind. So, it's important to check on the majors that interest you to see what they actually mean today.

Talking with people on campus is the best way of finding out what a major means today. Read material, especially, the college catalog, but do not rely on this. You must talk with people because the material may be out of date. Some of the courses listed may have been dropped since the last printing or may be offered only occasionally. The faculty may have voted just last week to change a major or a course, and the material you are reading will be incorrect.

Guides to the Territory

Knowledgeable people are your guides to the territory. Talking with one or two isn't sufficient; you need to talk with students, admissions counselors, and, if possible, people in the department in which your major is offered. Usually, these people are readily available and give talks during college visits. Go up to each one and talk, even if this person hasn't given a talk about the major you are considering. This will give you experience in talking with professors and wider exposure than you had before as to what different majors mean.

Develop Patience

Many students become unnecessarily impatient with themselves in the process of choosing a major. They become panicked when they see classmates in their senior year in high school confidently declaring what they are going to be doing for the rest of their lives. How can a high school senior know this? The employment gurus say that people, on average, will change their career seven times in their lives. A nurse returns to school years later and earns a doctorate in theology because she wants to offer spirituality in medicine; a West Point graduate and fighter pilot goes into his family's retail business but sells it at age 50 to get a law degree. People happily evolve into much more than they were as college students. They grow.

Peer pressure, however, saps patience. Seeing everyone running off with plans while you balance unsteadily on the decision seesaw causes stress. The problem with impatience is that it usually manifests itself in impatience with other people. And students need other people to help them find what major path they should follow.

Tips for Finding the Right Major for You

Staying focused on your search for a major involves being optimistic. Take nine optimism pills every morning. In addition, remember to:

- Cheer your friends on as they choose their majors, but remember that their decisions don't have anything to do with you. Their decisions are interesting but irrelevant.
- Set aside a time every week for thinking about your major, but don't obsess every day about the decision.
- Get organized in your search. Keep a notebook especially for information about majors.
- Notice how you make small decisions. Do you gather information and choose from among several options? Or do you choose the first idea that comes to you? Obviously, if you're doing the latter, you aren't taking advantage of all your options.
- Develop a sense of perspective. You aren't the first person who has had to choose a major or who has had difficulty with the decision.
- Keep looking for more information, more angles. These are speedy times, and facts and trends change very quickly. Be alert to changes.

The Prize Is Worth the Effort

No matter what major you choose, you will be better off than if you had never chosen one at all. College graduates today may start out in low-paying jobs but eventually do quite well. According to a report, "Education Pays 2004" (Sandy Baum and Kathleen Payea, College Board. 2004), in 2003, those workers with bachelor's degrees earned a median of $49,900. Those with a few years of college but no degree had median earnings of $35,700, while those with a high-school diploma earned a median income of $30,800. Over a 40-year career, the Board estimated, a college graduate is likely to earn about 73 percent more than a high school graduate.

College costs, but college pays.

CHAPTER 2

WHO AM I? TIME TO TAKE STOCK

Who are you? There are so many words that could be used. Are you: Spontaneous? Quiet? Adventuresome? Studious? Playful? Determined? Knowing yourself is the ultimate education. The more you know about yourself, the easier the task of choosing a major that fits with your interests, your abilities, your values, and your personal motivation will be. In this chapter, you will find ways of determining who you are.

Many factors contribute to who you are. Your genes (nature) determine a large part of who you are. Then the environment makes an impact (nurture). A current theory holds that genes may even determine happiness. According to this theory, the amount of happiness a person can experience seems to be set, with people always returning to their preset happiness level. Other studies have sought to demonstrate that shyness or a set weight is inherited.

Many people feel that environment, what you are exposed to as you grow up, greatly determines who you will become. Understanding as much as you can about yourself, including heredity and environment, is an important task. In choosing a college major, knowledge of yourself is key.

Many Tools Are Available to You

Our culture provides sophisticated tools for self-assessment. Some, which are described later, are formalized tests available at most schools at no cost. Here the emphasis is on what you can do on your own, a sort of a do-it-yourself project in self-discovery. Finding out about yourself is critical in deciding on a major.

Writing as Self-Discovery

Put "journaling " in your toolbox of self-discovery. It's not simply keeping a diary. In journaling, people write for many reasons: to establish contact with someone you no longer communicate with, to take your emotional temperature on any given day, or to slowly discover what it is that interests you most as far as a major is concerned.

As with any new activity, you might not feel that you are accomplishing anything at first. It takes time. Courses, conferences, and seminars are devoted to learning journaling. People learn how to record their thoughts and feelings to solve a particular problem or to gain insight.

Getting Started

For a month set aside a time every day or even just once a week to write what your feelings and thoughts are. Journaling will make you have a conversation with yourself. If you don't take the time to record what you are thinking and feeling, these thoughts and feelings get lost. Joan Didion, the American essayist, said,"I write entirely to find out what I'm thinking, and what I'm looking at, what I see and what it means. What I want and what I fear."

Find a comfortable, quiet place. Have a notebook and pen or pencil. If you prefer to work on a computer, that's fine. You may be surprised at what you find yourself writing. After about five weeks of doing this exercise, you will have a clearer picture of what your interests are or at least how you feel about different subjects.

The first prompt for the journal is:

Tell me about yourself.

Take time to follow this direction. Use scenes or incidents to describe who you are. Scenes you could include are:

The first day you went to school.
A really good day.
A funny thing that happened to you.

Or you could start by writing:

My friends say I am . . .
I've changed a lot in the last few years. I used to be . . .
When I wake up in the morning, I look forward to . . .
I hate it when . . .
Once upon a time . . .
During the day, I . . .
Time passes quickly for me when . . .
I like people who . . .
I was surprised when I found out . . .

Another way of discovering is by writing your name in big block letters. Then tell how your parents chose your name. If you don't know, try to find out.
Continue with these prompts:

My family likes to . . .
The most important thing I have learned from my mother is . . .
The most important thing I have learned from my father is . . .
When I am not working, I like to . . .
If I could ask one person an important question, I would ask . . .
If this person answered the question, he or she would say . . .
An ideal place for me to live would look like . . .
When I go to bed at night, I think about . . .
The classes I enjoy most are those that . . .
Five years from now, I can imagine myself . . .
I've always had a hunch that I would be good at . . .

Journaling requires that you write regularly about how you feel and what you imagine. This tool of self-discovery gives you time to really think about yourself. In the rush of a busy world, people forfeit time for self-discovery. Taking the time to journal will give you insight into who you are.

Here is what Joe Hirschmugl wrote in finishing the statement, "Despite how I seem on the outside, I am . . .

> . . . not as I seem. Regardless of what people see or hear when they ask me how I am doing, the truth is that usually I am not doing "fine." To me, the deception is obvious. Despite my words, I'm sure I am "telling" a different story. I'm sure I look away for a split second as I say I'm doing "good" or "great." I'm positive that my hands start to fidget and fuss. And I'm certain that I smile a brave smile that is unlike any expression I have when I'm really happy or content, one where my lips are pressed tightly together and the corners of my mouth turn upward, cutting into my cheeks. People don't see the person joking and smiling to protect himself from rejection and pain, the person talking because he's all too familiar with silence, the person who takes control because he knows what it's like to look forward to something and be disappointed. They don't see the person who never enjoys today because he's always working toward tomorrow, or the person all too aware of his shortcomings and the things he doesn't have.

In completing the journaling statement "I'm happiest when . . .," Jessica Canlas, an English major, wrote:

> I'm happiest when I feel as though I'm doing everything I can to maintain and improve myself and my well-being. Whether it be making sure I work out three times a week, making sure I get to church at least a few Sundays a year, or just something as simple as getting the oil in my car changed on time so that my engine doesn't explode—all of this stuff just adds up to me winning the war against one of my most formidable obstacles—laziness. And it's not just about getting up off the couch to change the channel instead of using the remote or making sure I get to work on time. I find myself becoming more and more preoccupied with bettering myself, learning new things, coming to a different understanding of the world around

me that some might call more "adultlike," but I consider it just putting my best effort into living a fulfilling life. None of us wants to end up old and gray, wondering about what could have been or what should have been done—but of course, I believe that that is almost inevitable. But at least I hope to be able to console myself with the fact that I tried my best when I was in school, that I tried my best to find a decent job, that I didn't TOTALLY squander what little money I had—and, most important, that I didn't push aside my dreams just to make life a little easier or to avoid the disappointment of failure. And that encompasses every aspect of life—physical, spiritual, emotional—just an all-around WHOLE-FEELING existence.

Read your writing after several weeks and determine what it tells you that you didn't know. On many individual days you will be slightly startled at what you write. Try to step back from the writing and see the you who might be submerged in the outward activity of life. Then, ask yourself these questions (or journal them):

- What activities do I enjoy regularly?
- What kind of people do I enjoy being around?
- What do I value in these activities and these people?
- When do I like myself best?
- What am I good at?
- What activities do I want to try in the future?
- What motivates me to do something new?
- Have I tried anything new lately?
- What am I looking forward to?
- What can I imagine myself doing at a later time in life?
- What stops me from trying new ideas?

While the journal promotes knowledge of the inner you, another tool, the Personal Fact Sheet, will help provide you with the specifics of the outer you that may be long forgotten. Fill out the Personal Fact Sheet (copy it if you are using a library book) asking relatives besides your parents to provide details when needed. You will be totally surprised at the number of facts and stories you will discover by doing this.

Personal Fact Sheet

1. Name _____   Date _____
2. Date of birth _____
3. Place of birth _____
4. Mother's maiden name _____
5. Father's name _____
6. Mother's occupation _____
7. Father's occupation _____
8. Parents' places of birth _____
9. Parents' interests _____
10. Grandparents' names _____
11. Grandparents' places of birth _____
12. Grandparents' occupations _____
13. Grandparents' interests _____
14. Occupations of other family members (sisters, brothers, cousins, aunts, uncles)
    _____
15. Interests of other family members _____
16. Significant neighbors and their occupations _____
17. Description of a house or apartment your family occupies
    (occupied)_____
18. Description of a car your family owns (owned) _____
19. Organizations your family members belong to (used to belong to)
    _____
20. Description of a typical holiday _____
21. Weekend activities of your family _____
22. Pets your family owns (owned) and their distinguishing characteristics
    _____
23. Events that stand out in the history of your family _____
24. Accomplishments of members of your family _____

Minibiography

Writing a minibiography, five or ten pages, will help you discover new aspects of yourself. Start with a page containing all the facts you can discover. Some are easy; you already gathered them for your fact sheet. Also include the answers to the following questions:

Where were you born? At home? In a hospital?

What number child were you? Firstborn? Middle? Number six? Your birth certificate supplies much of this information. It's surprising how many people have never seen their birth certificate.

Were you adopted? If you were, the birth certificate your parents have may not be the original. Theirs may merely certify that they are your legal parents.

What time of day were you born?

What was going on in the world? Was the United States at war?

What were your parents' occupations at the time of your birth? Did they both return to work after you were born? Who took care of you?

What kind of community were you raised in? Did you live on a reservation, in an urban setting, in the suburbs, on a farm?

Which schools have you attended. (With the average American selling his or her home every seven years, most children transfer schools many times.)

Which school was your favorite? Why? Were you educated in public, parochial, or private schools?

Were you in the United States for the whole time you were growing up, or did you go to school overseas also?

During your growing-up years, how did you spend your spare time?

Did television play a big part in your homelife?

Was there a park nearby where children gathered?

Did you spend time learning skills, such as karate, piano, gymnastics, basketball, computers?

Did you come from a family that encouraged new experiences or that felt more comfortable with the tried and true? Write examples.

What were your brothers, sisters, and cousins interested in?

How did your parents spend their spare time?

How often did other people visit your home?

What has been your work experience? Write about how you happened to get each of your jobs. Did you have choices?

What has been your community involvement? Does your family take part in community or church activities on a regular basis?

It might take you some time to get these facts together. From them, a distinct picture of your life to date will emerge.

Now, add a couple of imaginary paragraphs to the minibiography. They will mention your college major and what you were involved in the first few years after college. An imaginary scenario might be:

> (Your name) chose anthropology as her (or his) major in college and after graduation worked for a nonprofit agency in Appalachia, providing social services. After two years she (he) decided she (he) wanted to become a doctor and took post-baccalaureate classes in the sciences to prepare for the MCAT (admissions tests for medical school). Now (your name) is studying medicine at (*make up the name of a school*).

Skills You Have Now

Many of the skills you have now will be sharpened as you move through college. Students are often reluctant to admit they know anything about their own skills. Ask yourself the following questions and write your answers on the blanks below:

What am I good at? _____

What examples do I have of this? _____

Have I been encouraged to develop what I am good at? _____

By whom? _____

What do I think I might be good at? _____

How can I find out? _____

Who can help me learn more about this? _____

What am I interested in? _____

Have I had much exposure to this subject? _____

How can I find out more about it? _____

My friends would say that I'm skilled at _____

My family would say that I'm skilled at _____

In high school, I got good grades in _____

My grades didn't reflect my skills because _____

Your Skill Profile

Look at the following list of skills and circle the ones you already have. Next, go through the list again and put an X next to the skills you want to develop.

Logic	Design
Attention to detail	Communication
Drawing	Writing
Mechanical aptitude	Reading
Creativity	Performance
Social abilities	Problem solving
Research	Daily living
Planning	Preparation
Language	Decision making
Discussion	Athletics

Select three skills from the list that you would like to develop:

1. _____
2. _____
3. _____

How are you going to develop these skills? Where can you get help developing these skills?

The I'm-Going-to-Do-It Principle

Most of skill development is the "I'm-going-to-do-it" principle. Once you have decided that you don't have a particular skill but would like to have it, you can start developing your aptitude for it.

What happens if you find that you have little or no aptitude for this skill? You move on to the next one you want to develop.

ONE STUDENT'S SOLUTION TO PERFORMANCE ANXIETY

When Dontrey started playing the clarinet in junior high school, she would become paralyzed with fear whenever her school had a band night. The band director was a kind person, but he needed everyone to play. Even at this young age, Dontrey knew she had to overcome her fear of performing. The price she was paying was too high: extreme anxiety with an upset stomach before the performance, exhaustion afterwards, and zombielike feelings the next day.

When auditions were held in high school for the play *To Kill A Mockingbird*, she tried out for one of the minor parts, got it, memorized her lines perfectly, and forced herself to perform. Building on her initial triumph over stage fright, she got a part in *Major Barbara* in her junior year, and in her senior year she played the part of the nun in *The Prime of Miss Jean Brodie*.

She did not major in drama or theater in college; she chose biology. The performance skills she had worked so hard to develop served her well in her senior year as a teaching assistant. She led a class of 20 students after the large, weekly 400-person lecture with a professor.

Values

Everyone has personal values based on their family, their community, their religious or nonreligious beliefs or affiliation, and their experiences. Values are an important part of deciding what major you will pursue. The major must reflect your values. If it doesn't, your life will be in conflict. The stereotypical case is the student who probably should be a liberal arts major, but decides to major in business, because this person has heard that people who major in business make more money than do liberal arts majors.

Answer the following questions in your journaling notebook to help define what your values are.

1. How would you describe a successful person? Based on this description, how successful have you been so far?
2. If supporting yourself and, in the future, a family were not a concern, how would you spend your time?
3. If you were offered a million dollars to give up one of your friendships, what would you do?
4. What do you hope to achieve in the years ahead?

5. Is there anything you would like to change about yourself? If so, what?
6. Have there been experiences or people who have changed or influenced your ways of thinking? What were the changes?
7. What do you value in other people?
8. What do you value about yourself?
9. What does your community value? (hard work? country club membership? saving money? supporting those in need? fair rules for everyone? universal education? etc.)
10. What does your family value? (getting ahead? looking good? frugality? social life? etc.)
11. Do you admire your parents' values? Why or why not?

The Three Parts as Tripod

Your choice of major sits on top of a tripod. Values, skills, and interests each form one of the legs. Each part must be represented, or the major will topple over. Try to think carefully about each of the three parts.

SYLVIA HAS SKILL BUT NO INTEREST

Sylvia is very good at math in high school and believes it serves a purpose in society. She also wants to work toward an important goal. However, she is not interested in studying math further. She wants to do something else but doesn't yet know what it is. In college, she is going to look into other areas and take a variety of courses in her freshman and sophomore years.

Interviewing Your Family

Because we interact on a daily basis with friends and family, we take a lot for granted about who they are and who we are in relationship to them. Students who interview family members and friends find that by actually sitting down with a person and taking notes, insights come that are not apparent in day-to-day living.

Consider asking people in your family to sit with you while you take notes about their lives and the relationships among family members. If you don't do this, a rich source of personal information will be lost.

Following are some of the questions you might ask, although there are many more:

1. How long has our family been in this country?
2. When our ancestors came here, what kind of work did they do?
3. Why did they settle in this part of the country?
4. Did they move a lot?
5. What physical characteristics do many of our family members have?
6. How have they been successful?
7. What are some of the best traits of our family members?
8. Have I met all our relatives?
9. If not, where are they and what are they doing?
10. Do you mind if I write to them?
11. What is a good way to find their addresses?
12. Why don't we have contact with them?
13. Do all our relatives practice the same religion?
14. What illnesses seem to run in the family?
15. What are the values of our family? What do we treasure?
16. Have people in our family gone to college?
17. What did they major in?
18. What career did they have after college?
19. Can you think of any career regrets in our family?
20. Have our relatives had many different jobs?
21. Do you know why they decided to change jobs?
22. How did those decisions work out for them?
23. Do you have any good advice to pass on?

Grandparents and great-grandparents are excellent sources of information about family traits and history. Parents may be less helpful in telling you about what has gone before because they may still be fairly young. Aunts, uncles, and cousins add special information because their memories will be different from those of your immediate family members.

After you have interviewed family members, a picture of your family will emerge. Perhaps many people in your family have owned their own businesses, some successfully, others not. Some families have many members in the sciences. Others have a tradition of finishing high school and then working with their hands. Knowing what has gone before is knowing what influences you and perhaps limits you in your choice of major. If no one in your family, for instance, has gone to college, much less considered majoring in history, you may feel uncomfortable and cave in to familial pressure to choose a "practical" major. Parents without college experience may resent your absence at family affairs because you have to study. "She's always in the room with the books," they complain, or they may not understand when it takes you five years to finish school. In these cases, the student acts as a catalyst for change. If one member goes to college, others in the family might consider it as well.

Family Traits

Many students say that they are different from their families. Others say adamantly that they don't want to be like members of their family. However, most people are like their families, even though they don't recognize the similarity. For example, they vote for the same political party their family has voted for, they buy the same type of products they had in their home; or they have or don't have pets, depending on the home they were raised in. When you're young, you may appear to be the opposite of your family, but as the years go by, the chances are great that you will see more similarities than differences.

> So in regard to mental qualities, their transmission is manifest in our dogs, horses and other domestic animals. Besides special tastes and habits, general intelligence, courage, bad and good temper etc., are certainly transmitted. With man we see similar facts . . . that genius, which implies a wonderfully complex combination of high faculties, tends to be inherited; and . . . that insanity and deteriorated mental powers likewise runs in families.
>
> —Charles Darwin, 1871

> One recent twin study of intelligence found that the correlation of intelligence measures between twins remains as strong throughout the life of the twins. This indicates that unique environment is less important than we might instinctively imagine, a disquieting thought for those parents who strive to ensure that their children get a good education.
>
> —Professor Michael Gill,
> Department of Psychiatry,
> Trinity College Dublin,
> "Genes and Mental Health,"
> a symposium October 2004

If many members of your family go into pharmacy, you need to realize that you are not obligated to follow in the family tradition. Just knowing what the composite of your family is will help you to know more about your choices. Listen to the voices, and draw your own conclusions.

Consider the story of Tonya. She is the first person in her family to go to college, and her aunts always tell her that she is a fool. They are making good money owning their own beauty shops and think that Tonya is wasting her time majoring in communications.

"What good is that going to do you?" they ask her at every family gathering. Her mother tells them to leave her alone, but their comments leave Tonya anxious about whether she's made the right choice, whether she'll be able to pay off her student loans, and whether she is putting on airs just because she's in college. She doesn't know any of the answers yet, but this family does not value a liberal arts degree. Its value system is the practical, the only one family members have ever known. (Tonya's mother encourages her; the aunts don't.) "Mom Matters: Maternal Influence on the Choice of Academic Major," by Jacqueline C. Simpson, in *Sex Roles: A Journal of Research*, May 2003.

Family Traits Tree

Most of us have filled out a family tree in school. Usually, family trees merely tell the names, birth dates, and death dates of our relatives. People interested in genetic diseases are now adding health histories to these trees. What we are going to add is family traits. Your cousin Ida's ability to braid hair beautifully and carefully, for instance, might indicate fine motor skills as well as the ability to focus and concentrate. Your Uncle Robert's ability to play a musical instrument without reading notes is noteworthy and unusual. Many times people seem more similar to an aunt or uncle than they do to one of their parents. So design your own family traits tree on the next page, indicating the main traits or skills members of your family have demonstrated. Try to talk to the elderly members of your family to find out about relatives who have died.

FAMILY TRAITS TREE

A STUDENT PROFILE

Anthony, a senior at a public high school on the West Coast, said this about his skills:

"Since I was about eight, my mother has let me cook with her. By the time I was 14, I was starting to be a better cook than she was. I'd look at recipes and see how they could be improved. I have a big appetite, like everyone else in our family. They are all happy when I cook. Along the way, I started growing herbs to go into my dishes because the fresh always tastes a lot better than those in a jar from the store. But then I started getting really interested in computers too, so now I only cook when I am starved. My father lent me the money to start my own computer company when I was 16. Right now I'm helping a restaurant owner make his operation more efficient with the help of computers. I know a lot about computers and a lot about food.

"I don't do well with subjects like English and history that require a lot of reading. I don't get good grades at school because I have so many outside interests. I'm looking at colleges that have strong computer majors and business courses. I guess one of my skills is curiosity, and another is that I can stay with something until it works."

The Total Picture

Take a good, long look at the composite you have formed by doing the exercises in this chapter and ask yourself:

- How am I like members of my family?
- How am I not like them?
- What skills do I have?
- What do I value?
- What am I interested in?
- What motivates me?
- Who am I?

CHAPTER 3

GUIDING LIGHTS

Think of climbing Mt. Everest, or the duo of Will and Grace. Rarely do people succeed without the help of others. As humans we were designed to live in supportive communities in which others encourage us as we stumble along our path.

When the human tribe was smaller, perhaps things were easier. Imagine that you were born in prehistoric times. Your choices were probably limited as far as a life's work was concerned. First of all, you wouldn't be doing it for very long; your life expectancy was much shorter than the life expectancy of today where people live well into their 70s and beyond. Perhaps the tribe thought you would be a good hunter, while others did the fishing. Or, perhaps you became the leader of the gatherers. Or you were asked to be in charge of keeping the fire burning all day for cooking and warmth. Probably these jobs were assigned based on the tribe's knowledge about people's skills.

Today, the tribe is much larger and, as a result, has complex systems set up for what you are going to do to contribute to its maintenance. First, you choose what you would like to do, get the education, and then compete in the workforce for the most rewarding job or the job that fits best with your skills and temperament.

College is the time when you part from your parents and become independent and capable of making your own decisions. Even people who live at home during their college years are separating from their parents, learning to think independently in their studies, and being responsible for their own schedules and deadlines.

To make sense of this huge system, you need help. Finding the courage to ask for help is sometimes the hardest part. One of the reasons we have to ask for help today is that no one can know everything. Hunches, guesses, and gossip about your major are not going to be helpful. You need up-to-date facts from people whose job it is to gather these facts. You also need advice from people who are actually in the major field you are considering.

So take advantage of any kind of light that can be thrown on the subject, a headlight, a beacon, a votive candle, a searchlight, and starlight. Below is a star chart of all the guiding lights that will help you in your search for a major.

Searchlights: High School Guidance Counselors

Some students are afraid to go to the door of their high school guidance counselor. Planning for college admittedly is a big step. What do you have to lose? If no one went in to see them, these people wouldn't have a job. So you're doing them a favor by showing up. Think of it that way. You may go to a small high school at which not many people go on to college. Your school may be one in a suburb of a large city where most of the students think they should go to college, and the high school admissions counselor seems overworked. Whatever the situation, these are the people designated to know the most about getting into college.

Most high school counseling offices are crammed with materials from every college that hopes to recruit students from that school. There are also directories giving the addresses of lesser-known schools that might not usually recruit at your school. Many offices have computers that enable you to search for information on the schools in which you have an interest.

Be patient with the counselors. They may see hundreds of students in a week. The first time you visit may not be perfect. They don't know you yet. Go back again, a second and third time. If they have seen your face once, they will be more receptive when they see it again. It's an old cliché, but the squeaky wheel does get the oil. Eventually, as they get to know you and have a sense of what you need, they will have a personal interest in your success.

One way to prepare yourself for talking with the guidance counselor is to prepare a sheet of paper with basic information about you on it. Here are facts you might list:

Name

Year you're in at school

Favorite subjects so far

Extracurricular activities

Clubs

Outside interests

Foreign languages

Musical instrument

Special talents

Subjects you want to explore

Parents' occupations

Number of siblings and what they do

Ideas for after high school

Geographic desirability for colleges

Financial support for college

Next, make a list of questions you have for the counselor. It's normal to be unsure about what you're doing at this stage of the game. The counselors are trained to help students find answers to their questions. The process doesn't seem as complicated to students with older brothers or sisters at college. If you ask older siblings, they might give you good advice.

Some high schools require freshmen to accumulate personal information in a folder, which is for guidance counseling. As new information about the students is available, such as the results of interest inventory tests, the folder grows. During the four years of high school, the folder begins to resemble a CSI (Crime Scene Investigation) file. When you look at your folder, you will see how your thinking about college and majors has evolved over the four years.

When you meet with the counselor, be prepared. If you genuinely are at a loss concerning what major to choose, pick three even vaguely interesting majors. Prepare a list of about ten schools. Then, the counselor will have a basis for conversation. Most students choose schools that are geographically close to where they live. They don't want to travel thousands of miles to get home, plus they want to take advantage of the lower tuition for state residents at the state schools.

Be a Detective

If your high school is understaffed in this area, you will need to do much of the detective work on your own. Even though your schedule is already crammed with school work and outside interests and activities, you need to find the time to review not only what colleges you are interested in, but also whether they offer the subjects that interest you now.

Bookstores and libraries are filled with books that list statistics and information on colleges. Among those available are:

Barron's Profiles of American Colleges, Barron's Educational Series
Colleges That Change Lives: 40 Schools You Should Know About Even If You're Not a Straight-A Student, Loren Pope, Penguin
Peterson's Four-Year Colleges, Peterson Guides
The College Handbook, The College Board
Complete Book of College, The Princeton Review
The Insider's Guide to the Colleges, Yale Daily News staff, St. Martin's Press

Some guides are published by geographical region, and others offer information for specific groups, such as minorities and art majors.

Keep in mind that statistical information about a college does not present a clear picture for you. For example, numbers cannot tell you that a department in a college is going to be closed next year. Or you may be averse to attending a school that has a strong Greek system because of the emphasis on partying and superiority of cliques or that is not as supportive of female students as it is of male students. This type of information is found through word of mouth or on the Internet or by reading a book such as *The Insider's Guide to the Colleges,* compiled and edited by the staff of the *Yale Daily.* In addition, once you mention interest in a major to friends and family, you give them the opportunity to think of people they know who can supply additional information for you.

Looking at the Wide Field of Choices

Many students make the mistake of choosing a college based on its name recognition rather than its expertise in a particular field. If you were to look at the listings in *U.S. News & World Report's* annual

"America's Best Colleges," for instance, you might think that the top-rated schools offer every major you are interested in and that these schools excel in all fields. You may have an interest in gerontology, the study of aging, but you can't major in that at a small liberal arts college. Looking at individual departments, rather than at rankings of schools, is important in your selection.

In 1996 the press reported complaints that some colleges were providing one set of data to financial rating agencies and another to those writing guidebooks, publishing rankings, or providing college information for books and software. Now a standardized questionnaire has been written for the more than 40 kinds of data commonly requested by magazines such as *U.S. News & World Report* and *Money* magazine. This standardized form was designed to eliminate the problems of the past, such as including the scores of foreign students in average SAT scores or inflating the size of a college faculty by including part-time instructors. Even with the new form, the magazines do not have the resources to cross-check the information provided by the colleges. You need to look for books in the college placement office that actually rank departments within the schools you are considering.

The guidebooks are excellent resources for those who take the time to read and compare what different schools have to offer. Each guidebook offers slightly different approaches to looking at a school. Reading more than one will provide you with insight into the range of majors offered, majors that are most popular because of the reputation of the discipline at that school, and the amount of academic pressure. Some guidebooks spell out the academic pressure, while others merely cite the mean SAT and ACT scores, giving an indication of how tough or easy it is going to be to complete a program successfully.

Starlights: Your Hunches and Dreams

At this stage in your life it is extremely difficult to say with certainty what you want to major in and subsequently apply to your career. You are just "channel surfing." "I think we should celebrate the undecided student," said Sue Biemeret, the college consultant at Adlai E. Stevenson High School, a high-ranking high school in suburban Chicago. "Careers constantly change. I don't think you can know at 18 what to major in. That's why so many schools have a core curriculum of liberal arts courses. Students are required to study a variety of subjects in order to become intellectually well-rounded and to be exposed to a wide variety of subjects. Colleges do not expect students to have their futures all planned out freshman year. We try to put the emphasis more on learning the skill of decision making. This means they should be examining their academic strengths and weaknesses. They should think about what classes they liked most and liked least. They should be examining their values," she said.

Ms. Biemeret has been counseling students on college choices for many years. She said that it is extremely important for students to start making their own choices and not to rely on their parents to do the decision making for them.

Counselors not only teach how to "talk the talk" using the vocabulary and process of college admissions but also, and more importantly, provide guidance in how you can explore your dreams for the future and your hunches about what's right for you. The data on colleges can be overwhelming at times but the focus of exploring your personal intuitive sense of your own direction should not get lost in the blizzard of information in the counselor's office.

The Parent Factor

The next people to ask about majors are your parents. "It's amazing how many kids have no idea what their parents do for a living," said Sue Wendt, who has counseled many students at Lyons Township High School in LaGrange, Illinois, where 60 percent of the students are college-bound. "'My dad has some high pressure job and comes home crabby at night,' is typical of what students will say when I ask about their parents' jobs," she added.

The goal is not to have parents making the decision for you, but for parents to aid and support you in your decision. At the minimum, they supply another pair of eyes and ears to assess the information you are gathering. This is the ideal situation. However, some parents impede the process. At one end of the spectrum are the parents who don't want to become involved at all, for their own reasons. At the other end are parents who are too involved, potentially inhibiting your efforts in decision making. Many parents have not gone to college, and, for those who have, the college experience is completely different today than it was when they were in school.

Sometimes it takes a while for parents to accept the fact that a four-year institution is not the best way for everyone to get an education. Career-oriented colleges and universities prepare students for success in in-demand career fields. They offer training toward a specific skill and usually cost less than traditional colleges. The focus of these schools is applied education, in which students learn by doing. Typically, degrees are offered in business and technology.

"Our students are more pragmatic and career-focused. Foremost, they are interested in a broader educational experience and learning skills they can apply in the workplace," said John Skubiak, president of DeVry University, which is owned by DeVry, Inc., a publicly traded company.

Students at these technical colleges can start taking classes in their major right away and can finish college degrees quickly because of year-round classes. At DeVry most finish their bachelor's degrees within three years at a cost of around $50,000 (2005 tuition level). DeVry says that more than 91 percent of its graduates are employed in their fields within six months of graduation.

Time-Out

Parents might be fearful, of their daughter or son taking time off before going to school. When a student is unenthusiastic about the prospect of going to college and would prefer to work, a time-out might be the best option. The book, *Taking Time Off: Inspiring Stories of Students Who Enjoyed Successful Breaks from College and How You Can Plan Your Own* (College Admission Guides, Princeton Review), by Colin Hall and Ron Lieber offers first-person accounts from people who have taken an extended break before or during college. To find resources for planning a time-off, ask your high school college counselor or the advising office of your college. Consulting firms, such as the Center for Interim Programs in Boston (interimprograms.com), are in the business of providing help with planning time off in a variety of opportunities, such as living and volunteering at an ashram in Bali or a work-study program at a medicinal herb farm in the southern United States.

Another group of parents is adamant that their children know what they're going to do with their degree before they even start. This is where the campus visits are helpful. Going around a campus with a guide, an upperclass student, or other families serves to educate everyone about the college process. Parents will see that most students have only a vague notion of what they want to major in. A student not knowing is more common than the parents suspected.

Whatever category your parents fall into, it is best to begin talking with them about your considerations. You are being educated about schools, and they will be too. Gathering information and sharing it is the first step.

Enlightenment: Career Days and Nights

Almost every large college campus sponsors career days at which students have a chance to interview companies for jobs. There's a lot to be learned at these events. Even if you attend a smaller school, it is still possible for you to attend a career day. The schools planning these events put ads in the newspapers and on the radio. Call and see if all students are welcome.

Don't be shocked at the dressed-for-business attire of students attending. No one being interviewed for a job wears a baseball hat backwards. Students all carry around their résumés, shake hands with interviewers, and look like they are under severe stress. Usually the event is staged in a gymnasium or auditorium, and students may go from table to table to hear about the individual companies. Go to one of these events long before you are scheduled to work in the outside world. Talking with the company personnel, usually from the human resource departments, gives you an opportunity to hear the language, get used to the dynamics, and see what majors companies are hiring.

Recruiters appreciate the students who come up to the table, shake hands confidently, and say what they are interested in doing. If you don't know yet, you can mention the areas that interest you. You will be amazed at the information these people have to share. They know trends, salaries, educational requirements, the culture of the organization they represent, and many other aspects of working.

Usually the fair organizers have set up a space at one end for company representatives to interview prospective employees. They can quickly tell if the student is the kind of person and has the skills the company is looking for. Or they may ask the student to come to an interview at the company.

The energy at a job fair or a career day is high because some students are hopeful that they have made a good connection and may get hired. Students bring copies of their résumés and take notes to read later. At rest areas around the room students congregate and share the information they have gathered about the companies. By the end of the day, everyone who attends is exhausted because there are so many possibilities and only a short time to pursue each one.

Even if you are a long way from graduation, career days are useful for you to attend. Recruiters who have spare time are eager to be busy and talking to students. They understand that some students are just fishing and not serious about job hunting yet. Use this time to gain information for yourself about career paths.

Beacons: Information Interviews

One of the best ways to find out about a potential career is to ask a working professional for an interview. These specifically are called "information interviews," and working professionals are familiar with the term.

Normally, the word *interview* scares students, but, in this form, students are seeking information rather than an actual job. They go out and conduct the interview with people in business or industry who are willing to give a half an hour or more of their time to talk about what they actually do at work and what they see as the future for their industry.

It's difficult, perhaps, to imagine why a working person would take time out of his or her busy day to be interviewed by a student. Still, many do agree to do this. Some have signed up with the alumni office of their colleges as willing volunteers for such interviews. Others are flattered when a young person calls. Many people who are in responsible positions feel they have an obligation to educate people about their company and industry.

Sources of information interviews can be found in many places, even on the bus ride on the way home. You may strike up a conversation with the person next to you, and he or she gives you a business card. Great! Chance meetings may provide many networking opportunities in the future.

It is never too early to start practicing this very valuable exercise. The main skill this requires is initiative. You must decide to call people and ask them to give you some of their time.

A low-stress information interview, such as one with a neighbor or a friend at his or her place of work is a good way to start. Besides people you know, make a list of ten people or organizations you might call. You also can get names of companies or organizations from the library.

The human resources (HR) department of an organization keeps all records of employees. Movies and action videos generally don't star the people in HR, but these hardworking people placers can be extremely good sources of information about the people you need to see.

Make up your list with phone numbers and enough space after each person's name or after each organization for notes.

This has to be regarded as a skill-building campaign. People who have never had an interview or conducted an interview don't do as well as those who have become familiar with the process. The earlier you start, the better.

The first call is often the most stressful. After that you will become a pro. Your most important tool is the phone. You may be nervous at first, but you will gradually get better. You might have a script in front of you, like the ones that telemarketers use (see below). This script can be used whether you are calling the human resources department of a company or are calling the person you want the interview with. Remember, you may have to make eight phone calls before you get a nibble. Don't take any of the negative responses personally. People are rushed sometimes, don't understand the request, or are unfamiliar with the process. You will get better the more times you do this.

Script for Information Interview Request

Hello, Mr. (or Ms.)_____. My name is _____. I am

_____
(name, year, and school). I got your name from _____, and I'm calling to get information about the field of _____
(the person's career field). I am not looking for a job, but I would greatly appreciate hearing about your work experience in the field of _____
(name the area this person works in). I would appreciate 20 minutes of your time and am available as early as 7:30

any morning. (This statement will really impress the person. Many busy people start work early, and if you meet with one then, you will not be interrupted by phone calls and other problems. Plus, suggesting this early time means you are really a go-getter.)

The person you are calling might readily agree or might put you off because he or she is very busy. If people can do it, fine. If not, politely thank them and move on to the next person on your list.

Once you have set the time, date, and place for the interview, start doing your homework. You must have a list of prepared questions. Students watch television interviewers such as Oprah or Matt Lauer, who make it seem effortless. Both these television personalities are hard workers who also have researchers to look up information for them and help them prepare their lists of questions. They can't possibly know all the details of the lives of the many people they interview. Who can remember off the top of his or her head how old Madonna is? Or how many Oscars went to *Million Dollar Baby*? Pros have to do research and be prepared, just as you do.

A list of 10 questions, written out, will be sufficient. Here are typical questions asked in these interviews. You can choose from among these or think of others that might be better for you:

What was your major in college?

How did you get this job?

How relevant was your major in getting this job?

How long have you been with this company?

What kind of training or education is necessary for your position?

What is the culture of the company? (Many professionals don't think about this question until an interviewer asks it. If the person you're talking to needs a prompt, ask what the values of the company are and how they are demonstrated on a day-to-day basis).

What do you actually do each day?

What hours do you work? Do you work evenings, weekends, or overtime? Are you compensated for extra time?

Do you have any travel in your job?

Are you part of a team?

If so, what is your role?

What is the best part of your job?

What is the worst part of your job?

How is your time divided between working with people, data, and technology?

What skills and talents are necessary for getting your job done?

How much variety is there in your work?

Do you get enough input from supervisors?

How much stress are you under?

How does the company motivate you?

How much contact do you have with people outside the company?

Are there any advantages or disadvantages in being a woman or a man in this job?

How is your industry changing?

Is there much social life with other employees?

What is the entry-level salary in this field?

If you had it to do all over again, would you major in anything different in college?

Is it important in your field to continue to take courses?

What do young people need to know about the world of work?

How relevant was your major in doing this job?

Does your company employ people who majored in a variety of different areas?

Is a master's degree required for people in your field?

Can you recommend other people who might talk to me about this field?

You can scribble the person's answers in a notebook, or, with permission, use a tape recorder. Tape recorders make many people nervous and hesitant to say what they are really thinking in response to your questions. Or you may just sit and listen attentively.

Besides preparing questions, a few other plans need to be made before the interview. Know exactly how to get where you're going and how long it will take to get there. In large metropolitan areas today, travel time may be extended by weather conditions, road construction, and accidents, so give yourself plenty of time. Plan on arriving 20 minutes early. Bring something to read so that you will not get restless.

A Perfect Opportunity for You to Use Your Good Manners

Dress neatly for the interview. When the person comes to the waiting room to meet you, stand up, shake hands, and say, "Thank you for your time," and refresh the person's memory about who you are and where you go to school. In this extremely busy world people appreciate review. Even though you might be nervous about conducting this interview, the person being interviewed might be nervous also. Even though you may feel as if you are just a lowly student who has been granted this enormous favor, the person being interviewed might feel a bit anxious about having to answer all your questions. Most people aren't interviewed every day and are as self-conscious as you about their grammar, their answers, and their diction. A good way to make everyone feel at ease is to have your questions prepared, tell the person how many you have, and tell him or her at various points how far along you are in your questions. "My sixth question out of the ten I have prepared is. . ."

At the end of the interview tell the individual how much you have appreciated his or her time and information. Be specific; say what impressed you or what you learned. Manage your interview so that it lasts 20 minutes or so. You may be encouraged to stay longer, but do not stay beyond 30 minutes. The person you're meeting with is busy. Respecting other people's time is a sign of maturity. Time is scarce, and everyone appreciates consideration of this valuable resource. If there is a secretary or receptionist who helped to set up the interview, remember to thank this person also on your way out.

Here are some obvious points to keep in mind during the interview:

- Don't chew gum.
- Don't light up a cigarette.
- Don't touch anything on the person's desk.
- Offer to excuse yourself if a phone call comes in, but don't lose your train of thought.

If, for some reason, you arrive for the interview and the person can't meet with you, politely ask to reschedule. People may be called out of town; they get sick; there can be many reasons for a cancelled interview. It happens. Don't let this temporary setback stand in your way. Schedule another time for another interview. *Or ask if there is anyone else you could meet with, as long as you are already there.* Some people are willing to substitute for missing colleagues.

Write a thank-you note immediately upon returning home. Below are common scripts.

> Dear (Mr. or Ms., not Miss or Mrs.):
>   The time you spent with me on (insert day) was extremely helpful in broadening my knowledge of the field of (name area). I was impressed with (refer to something the person told you, such as the volume of sales of his or her company, the number of hours required each week at work, the variety of tasks required each day).
>   Thank you again for your time.
>
>   Yours truly,
>   Signature
>   Your name typed
>   Phone number

Or you might write a note such as this one,

> Dear (Mr. or Ms., not Miss or Mrs.):
>   Thank you very much for the interview you gave me last (day of week). As a student trying to decide on a major, I find it extremely helpful to hear how others have made this decision and how it translates into the world of work.
>   Thank you again for your time.
>
>   Yours truly,
>   Signature
>   Name typed
>   Phone number

Today some people follow up interviews with a thank-you e-mail. A typed or handwritten note takes more effort on your part but it will make a more lasting impression on the recipient. The main point is to get it done. There are two advantages to doing it right away:

1. You won't have the nagging feeling that you should be writing a thank-you note.
2. The person will see your name once again and is apt to remember you as a polite, well-organized individual should your paths ever cross in the future, particularly after college when you will be using all the contacts you have ever made to land a job.

For your own benefit, type or write the results of the interview. Your impressions right after the interview of what the person said will seem dramatically different six months later when you are reviewing all your interviews.

Your Reactions to the Interview

Suppose you interviewed an accountant because that's the field you are considering majoring in. You may have three different reactions to the interview:

1. You may be excited because the job seems even more desirable than you had imagined; you hadn't realized before the interview that accountants today have as much interaction with clients as they do.
2. You may feel dazed because you realize that there's a lot more you need to find out about what different fields of accounting involve before you decide to major in this field.
3. You may feel discouraged because you didn't like what you heard and can't imagine yourself working in this field based on what this person told you

Regardless of whether the answer is 1, 2, or 3 from this list, you must conduct more information interviews. You shouldn't draw conclusions on the basis of just one interview.

If your reaction was number 1, you may need to check to make sure that the person you interviewed wasn't painting too rosy of a picture of the field of accounting. He or she might have unconsciously been trying to lure you to this field by minimizing the negatives.

If your reaction was number 3, it's time to look at other fields in addition to the one you've been considering. Consider yourself very fortunate at this stage because many people don't realize until their first month on the job what they have actually gotten themselves into. And this means lawyers, doctors, and people with doctorates in every field. They are stunned to find out all sorts of things about the work situation that they couldn't have known merely by going to school.

Regardless of whether your reaction was 1, 2, or 3 from the list, you must conduct more information interviews. You shouldn't draw conclusions on the basis of just one interview.

Information interviews are more crucial today than ever before because fields are changing so quickly. And every job is enormously specialized. Different areas of the country offer different types of jobs in the same field. Only by going out as your own career reporter can you find what you need to know. And high school is not too early.

Take Advantage of Interviews

Many people you ask to interview will be receptive to you. It gives them a chance to give back to a young person and gives them a break to think about what they are actually doing at work.

Take what every person says to you with a sense of skepticism or a grain of salt. You are getting the view of only one person in one field, and there are thousands of others. You may interview this person when he or she is having a really good day or a really bad day. Most people are very conscientious about conveying information to suggestible young people, but you have to remain objective. If you interview five accountants, and they all tell you that they have a great deal of client contact in their work, then you can be reasonably sure that this is a major aspect of being an accountant today. And if five pharmacists say they feel they are serving an important need by providing important drug information and a friendly face when people aren't feeling well, you can be reasonably confident that this represents the field.

The danger lies in interviewing only one person and drawing conclusions from that interview that may or may not be correct. If you were a newspaper reporter, you would have to check any statements made to you by people you interview. Consider your source's comments an open door to a room. Go in and look at its contents more closely. Give yourself enough time to look at the room; don't scurry around and exit before you've noticed all the furniture, the carpeting, the lighting, and the space. How does the room look? How does it feel when you're in it?

Many seniors in college conduct information interviews before they enter the job market. Occasionally, they get a job offer as a result of the interview even though this is not what was planned. Information interviews are a great way to network, one of the skills that is discussed later in this book. The more people you know, the greater your sources of information about the world. Information interviews are a passport to greater experience and awareness of the world, but many people are too frightened to try this harmless and cost-free way of getting ahead. The younger you are when you start doing them, the greater your rewards will be.

One Student's Impressions from a Speechwriter

Irene O'Donnell, an English major, wanted to know what was involved in being a speechwriter. She wrote the following report after her information interview:

> This past week I interviewed Ms. Angeline Harris,* a woman with extensive experience in speechwriting. She passed along some very enlightening information about this field, which I will summarize.
>
> Speechwriting for money never occurs right away, and according to Ms. Harris, most speechwriters never intended to work in this area for a living. Instead, it usually happens as an offshoot of something else.
>
> The two career paths that lead to this field are politics or public relations. By following a candidate for some time in another capacity or working as a political journalist, political speechwriting can eventually follow.
>
> The majority of corporate speechwriting happens in the PR department. Ms. Harris advised starting out at a large agency with a variety of clients to develop the kind of experience that can lead to speechwriting. However, even with a great résumé Ms. Harris told me that once she began writing speeches on a freelance basis, it was still very difficult for her to gain contacts and further

* Not person's real name.

work outside of the clients she maintained from her PR job.

In order to write a good speech, she said one needs to be able "to write a good promotional schtick." She finds speechwriting unfulfilling and views it more as a way to increase her income. She suggested browsing through trade journals about PR and business writing on the Internet for more information.

On a different note, Ms. Harris told me that although she earned a fantastic salary working in the PR field, she found it extremely unsatisfying. She described such work as, "Not the way writers would naturally live," and advised me to take care; that as an English major, whatever I start out my career in, I will very likely become quite stuck in. Several years down the road, changing my career would be extremely difficult, if not virtually impossible. She encouraged me to strive for personal satisfaction before salary. If I do that, she was confident that I would be fine. On a final note, Ms. Harris told me that if I wanted to do an internship at her former PR company, which has an office here in Chicago, she would put in a good word for me.

Testing

Wouldn't this all be easier if you could just take a battery of tests to tell you what you are good at and what you want to do? It would be exquisitely easy, but research on even the most widely used tests for aptitude and interests say that the tests are not entirely correct. They are a tool and provide a basis for decisions, but they do not reflect your intuitive sense of what the best path is for you.

However, many tests are available free, either at the high school guidance office or in the career counseling office of the college you attend or are thinking of attending.

For example, the nationwide Johnson O'Connor Research Foundation offers testing for 18 distinct aptitudes and compares the results with aptitudes required in hundreds of different careers. The cost for seven hours of testing and one and a half hours of evaluation is $600 (jocrf.org). The company says that its assessment measures inherent abilities that have little to do with knowledge, culture, interests, or experience.

Myers-Briggs Type Indicator

The Myers-Briggs Type Indicator (MBTI), or the Myer-Briggs, as this test is popularly called, has been taken by thousands of students and professional people, as well as members of unions and homemakers. Designed by two American women, Katharine Briggs and her daughter, Isabel Briggs Myers, the MBTI tests and analyzes your personality. Using 4 personality preference scales and 16 distinct personality types, the test helps you discover how your personality fits into the world of school and work. Myer and Briggs based their work on the discoveries of Carl Jung, an eclectic psychoanalyst and disciple of Sigmund Freud. Principally, the test will help you discover your motivations and preferences. Once these are discovered, finding an appropriate major and job is much easier. You may not be surprised by the results; they probably will verify what you already know about yourself.

The MBTI personality assessment deals with four aspects of personality:

1. How you interact with the world and where you direct your energy: extrovert or introvert.
2. The kind of information you normally notice: sensing or intuition.
3. How you make decisions: thinking or feeling.
4. Your preference for living: judging or perceiving.

After someone qualified to administer the test has tested you, you will be given a four-letter label for yourself. The letters are: E (Extrovert); I (Introvert); S (Sensing); I (Intuition); T (Thinking); F (Feeling); J (Judging); P(Perceiving). Once the results of the test indicate your personality type, the counselor will review what career options are best for you.

Some college counseling centers offer group sessions to people who have taken the test to analyze the results and hear what the individual sets of letters mean.

Strong Interest Inventory

The Strong Interest Inventory (SII) is the most widely used test for vocational assessment. Administered at both high schools and colleges, and for adults, it was first published in 1927 by E. K. Strong and was rewritten most recently in 1994. Consisting of 317 items, the test asks the taker to evaluate his or her preferences for different occupations in a like/indifferent/dislike format. Your counselor at school can explain the test and help you evaluate the results.

Computerized Testing Services

Many campuses offer computerized programs that you can access at your leisure to determine your career path. One that is used on many campuses is called SIGI-Plus (System of Interactive Guidance and Information Plus More). Colleges offer SIGI-Plus to their students as an interactive aid for the main aspects of career decision making and planning. The first section of the test introduces you to the program and outlines what it will do for you. Next, you must answer questions about your self-awareness: "What do I want?" "What am I good at?" This part of the test helps you decide what's really important to you by identifying your most important values, interests, and skills. Next, the test focuses on occupations. You can choose from a menu the characteristics you want in your work and what you want to avoid in your work. The program then lists occupations that match what you asked for. This part helps you to select a college major and provides you with a list of related occupations.

You can also choose hypothetical occupations for yourself, and the program tells you what skills these occupations require. It also gives you a chance to rate yourself on these skills. In addition, it informs you of typical preparation paths to the occupations. Finally, the program gives you a plan of action in light of what you have discovered by answering all the questions.

Independent Educational Consultants

On the Internet you can find the names of independent educational consultants who specialize in the college choice process. Their fees range from $1,500 to $5,000 depending on the area of the country. They review transcripts and test scores, recommend test preparations, if needed, and answer questions about majors and what colleges have to offer. They also help students develop ideas for essays.

The good consultants visit several colleges a year, meeting with administrators to discover changes in curriculum and what the colleges expect of students. "We're the ones who warn students not to blow off senior year," said Sue Bigg, a consultant in Chicago.

CHAPTER 4

TASKS TO JUMP-START YOUR SEARCH

Letting a major come bubbling to the surface without effort on your part is similar to playing craps with your future. With a small amount of work each semester on choosing a major, you will be armed to make the right choice. "I wish I had known" are words of futility after you have spent four or more years on a subject only to find you would have been happier with another major. And remember, a major isn't forever.

A Working Calendar for High School Students

Freshman Year. Your high school may have an advising program that starts in freshman year. However, the main task for you in this first year is to adjust to high school. So much is new—you may never have changed classes before or are surprised at how much is expected of you. Just finding the right people to have lunch with can be stressful. Whatever discomfort level you experience this year, keep in mind that it will get better. Concentrate on learning how to learn. Most students gain expertise in studying during this year. As you learn how to study, your grades will improve. If you have time, joining school clubs offers a way to meet new people and to find people to study with.

Sophomore Year. The least stressful of all four years of high school, this year provides you with a good opportunity to learn how to interact with teachers. If you have not yet met the guidance counselors, now is the time to introduce yourself. While freshman year was a time of disorientation, most sophomores are beginning to feel more confident and more able to talk with teachers and other people to gain information. The sooner you learn this skill of reaching out to people who have more experience than you, the quicker you will find useful information.

This is a good year to try different activities. If you have always been very active socially, you might try some quiet pursuits that you can accomplish on your own. If you've always been a solitary person, this is the year to spread your wings. Take some chances; try talking to people you haven't talked with before. They may surprise you. If they don't seem interested in talking, move on to someone else. Their loss.

Be alert to news of college fairs, programs on college admissions, and books or magazine articles about people in professions that are of interest to you. And if you haven't seen the movie *Napoleon Dynamite,* rent it. The characters in this movie are high school students who creatively overcome family dysfunction, loneliness, and shyness.

Junior Year. In your junior year, your life will be dominated by tests. You will probably take the SAT I and/or the ACT in the spring and the SAT II, if it's required by the schools you are considering. You will be taking the PSAT/NMSQT, which may qualify you for National Merit Scholarship awards. Some students take the PSAT during their sophomore year to get a headstart on career counseling. The test taken in sophomore year will not qualify you for National Merit Scholarship awards.

You might be scheduled for a meeting with your guidance counselor to review your transcript and standardized test scores. At this meeting you will learn which colleges may consider accepting you. College representatives will be making the rounds. This is a good time to ask them about specific programs that interest you.

Other students will start talking about where they are thinking of going to college. At a school where many students are college bound, the jockeying for status positions starts early. At schools where few are going to college, the decision is difficult because there are few other students with whom you can share ideas and information. If possible, schedule trips to campuses on days when schools are in session. Start listening more carefully to people already out of college. Ask them questions about their jobs. Ask what they majored in in college. A good question to ask is whether they would major in the same subject again.

Senior Year. Senior year is a scramble. Use the summer before your senior year by spending time reading about what different colleges have to offer in majors. Also spend time reading about the majors in different books, magazines, and by checking for this information online. Read the *Occupational Outlook Handbook* compiled by the U.S. Department of Labor, Bureau of Labor Statistics. The government gathers information from trade associations, professional societies, unions, and industrial organizations to provide up-to-date information on jobs and the projections of employment in these jobs from 2005–2010. The highlights of the government's information are provided in Chapter 10 of this book.

Be sure to look also at Chapter 7 in this book called "New, Unusual, and Design-Your-Own Majors." Then look at the colleges you are considering to see if they provide you with a wide choice of alternatives.

A Working Calendar for College Students

Having a schedule of what you need to do each semester will help you advance toward your goal.

Freshman Year. This will be a time for you to familiarize yourself with the school and what it has to offer. In addition to orienting yourself to life on campus, you should do the following:

1. If electives are available to you, consider studying something you have had no exposure to, such as psychology.
2. Find out where the career counseling center is on campus. Just know where it is, you don't have to go there.
3. Build your social skills so that you can to talk to people easily and can get valuable information from them.
4. Read newspapers and magazines and note what jobs people do and what the stories tell you about the jobs.

Sophomore Year. Now that everything has settled down and you are actually accustomed to being a college student, you can do the following:

1. Review all the courses offered at your college. This sounds like an amazingly simple and time-wasting exercise, but you will be surprised at the diversity and richness of courses offered at most colleges and universities today. Like the rest of the population, students frequently suffer from nearsightedness, only focusing on what interests them. It's important to review all your options.
2. Find upperclass students who are majoring in the subjects you are considering pursuing. They will tell you the realities of the course of study.
3. Even if your mind is made up about your major, consider the course sequences for two others. Also, consider what you might want to minor in. Minors frequently are overlooked and can be a source of great interest.
4. Find out who does the advising at your school. Make an appointment with this person early in your second semester. The school may already have you scheduled to see the adviser sometime during the year. Be sure you bring a notebook and have many questions prepared. Advisers are extremely busy, and you want to make the most of the time you have with the one you're meeting with.
5. Play the "what if . . ." game with yourself. "What if I majored in geology and minored in business?" The purpose of this exercise is to discover what kind of expertise this will give you after you finish college.
6. Declare your major and minor or your double major. Register for as many courses as you can in your major and minor for the summer and fall. By taking advanced courses early, you will be able to determine whether you have made the right choice or not.

Junior Year. You're now taking your major and minor courses. This is a time for evaluation and assessment. Be sure to do the following:

1. Work very hard in your courses so that your grade point average in your major is high. Employers frequently ask potential employees about their overall grade point average and the grade point average in their major.

2. Start getting to know the professors in your major department by stopping in during office hours and asking them questions. The main purpose is twofold: to gain information and for them to remember you when it comes time to write letters of recommendation for jobs or graduate school. Often no one shows up during office hours to talk to instructors, so they are available. Take advantage of this. They have a wealth of information about their fields, and most are willing to share if students show an interest. Inquire about research projects they are doing that you could possibly become involved in.

3. Find out how students participate in internship or cooperative education projects at your school. Sign up for one during the year and one next summer.

4. Be alert to people with your major who are working so that you may interview them about their jobs.

5. Go to job fairs to get an idea of what is being offered.

6. Check with your major adviser to make sure that you are taking the courses required in your major for graduation.

Senior Year. At this point, you should know where you're going and what you want. It's time to do the following:

1. Make an appointment early in the year with the career counseling center on campus.

2. Conduct information interviews with people in your field who are working.

3. Spend sufficient time to write an impressive résumé and have someone critique it for you.

4. Collect names of people you can use as references in your job search or faculty members who are be willing to write letters of recommendation for you for graduate school, if you're planning to go.

5. Go to job fairs to familiarize yourself with what opportunities are available for you and to distribute your résumé to prospective employers.

6. Master the art of writing cover letters to go with your résumé. These letters are a sales tool that will help convince prospective employers of your desirability as an employee. The most impressive ones demonstrate that a potential employee has researched the company and can contribute to the company. Many prototypes are listed on the Internet. Personalize and individualize yours.

This rough outline of a calendar for four years should give you an idea of the time when each major task should be accomplished.

Other Missions to Accomplish

In addition to these calendars to keep you on track, there are lots of other things you can do to make sure you have all the information you need to choose the right major.

Building Networks

If you hang around with only your roommate from freshman year to graduation (highly unlikely), you will not know much about what the world of majors has to offer. Frequently, it's difficult to meet someone who is considering majoring in nursing if you are interested in engineering. Try to meet people with different interests. Your insight will expand, and your brain will connect with new ideas. Expand and grow.

Even if you are quite confident about what you want to study, exposure to other people's interests might make you change your mind. Frequently, students choose a major because of family pressure or underexposure to other fields available to them.

If you are naturally social and eager to meet others, you are already well on your way to meeting people on campus who will expand your thinking about majors. If you have not developed your social skills yet, college is a perfect time to start.

Where? On almost every campus there is a chance to meet new people in the cafeteria, on the shuttle bus stop, in the lecture hall, or by volunteering at the homeless shelter. Set a goal of trying to meet one new person a day. Most schools are in session about eight months of the year. Eight times 30 days equals 240 new people you could meet. What a wealth of information!

Learning Small Talk, How to Talk Small

Most conversations do not start with big ideas. Usually people start with small subjects like lunch, team scores, and the unreliability of the bus schedule. Then, after both people check out the other person's language use, level of sophistication, attitude, and other clues, the conversation either proceeds or it stops. Sometimes, it is merely a network time filler.

Small talk is extremely important in the process of getting information you need about your major and your subsequent career. Believe it or not, people will judge your sophistication by how well you are able to talk about nothing of importance. Frequently, this talk revolves around sports, the weather, or food. Other popular topics are trying to stay in shape, developments on *CSI*, and overspending on credit cards. Almost everyone in the United States knows something about one of these topics. Ramifications of winning the lottery also ignite conversations.

College is a great place to start practicing the art of saying nothing of substance. People will then judge you worthy to go on to the next step of more important topics.

Listen to the small talk that goes on around you every day.

"I can't believe it's snowing, and I still don't have boots."
"I don't either, but I'm maxed out on my credit cards and can't buy any right now."
"Hey. How's the semester going?"
"Not too bad, but I have this calculus class that's a killer."
"Hi! What's happening?"
"Not much, but I got a flat tire on the way to school today."

Imagine that you have to add the third sentence to any of these exchanges. In what direction could you go?

Most small talk involves keeping the tennis ball in the air, quite often effectively by merely asking a question that hinges on the last statement. By listening to what other people say, you can easily develop a repertoire of small talk. Just copy.

Bypassing Procrastination

Procrastination equals perfectionism. Procrastinators have huge imaginations of how grand any project could be, but they don't get started because they can never attain such heights. As one junior remarked, "I finally figured it out. It doesn't matter how smart you are. What matters is whether you can stay on top of everything that needs to get done." A sure way not to stay on top is to avoid doing tasks because you have imagined how extraordinary they have to be. Settle for ordinary. If you have extra time, then maybe you can try for extraordinary. Avoid the procrastination trap.

Doing Your Homework on Majors

Choosing a major requires your doing homework. Like the homework you've been doing since second grade, it requires preparation, organization, and attack! The college admissions office at your high school has several books that list the facts about colleges. You may decide to buy one so that you can review it at home. As you look through it, jot down the names and addresses of the schools that interest you. In addition, your adviser may have some information about the schools that is not apparent from the books.

College Catalogs

Try as they will, not all information that colleges post on their Web sites is up to date. Some have disclaimers:

> This document is for informational purposes only and does not constitute a contract. Every effort has been made to insure accuracy, but be advised that requirements may have changed. Errors may have also been introduced in the conversion to an html document. Thus for items of importance, it might be wise to seek confirmation in the paper version or directly from the appropriate campus office

Keep a list of the catalogs you have requested. Depending on the time of year your request is made, delivery may take as much as two months, but more typically it takes a month. As the catalogs come in, check them off your list. Writing your own scoring system of the schools is helpful. At the top of your grid, write or type the features that are important to you, such as geographic location, size, ratio of men to women, tuition, financial aid, and whatever else you have decided is important. On the left-hand side of the page, write the names of the schools.

Naturally, schools design their catalogs and Web sites to attract students. Almost as polished as advertising tools, information is presented in a way that will try to interest you in coming to the school. Following are some points to consider when you're looking at Web sites:

What has the school chosen to emphasize?

What majors does it offer?

Which majors are of interest to you?

What courses are listed under the major?

Do the course descriptions sound interesting?

What kind of people are in the pictures? Do the students in the pictures look like the kind of people you want to be with?

What is the spirit of the Web site? Is there just a nuts-and-bolts description, or are there interesting descriptions of the process of education?

The Library

The library is the repository for everything you ever wanted to know about majors. Talk with the reference librarian about the areas you want to search and the databases available to you. Many college libraries have special sections designed to help people find information about majors and their relationship to careers. In addition, libraries frequently keep hard copies of college catalogs.

Your Computer Screen

Most college Web sites now contain virtually all the information that is in their printed catalogs, and they are a great place to start your research into schools and majors that interest you. A school's Web site can easily be found through the use of a search engine like Google or Yahoo!. Not only will you be able see what departments and courses a school offers, but many Web sites offer a virtual campus tour so that you can check out what the campus is like.

The Crucial Campus Visit

After you have determined as much as you can by reading college materials online and in hard copy, prepare for a visit to the campus. Schools are eager to have you visit. Your visit should include more than following a talking guide around the buildings. You should request interviews with students and professors in the major you are considering. A campus visit will be much more meaningful if you actually get a chance to ask people questions about the subject you are considering studying. Use the techniques you learned earlier in the information interviews to help you prepare questions, such as the following:

What will I learn in this major?

What are the strengths of the professors in this major?

Do you know how a major at this school differs from the same major at other schools?

Are there opportunities for field study or internships?

Are classes in my major hard to get into?

What do students with this major do after they graduate?

What is the most difficult class in this major?

What are typical minors that students in this major have chosen?

Is there an opportunity to do an interdisciplinary major with this major?

Is there opportunity for foreign travel with this major?

With this major, how many years does it typically take to graduate?

What are the most popular courses in this major?

What skills do you need to have to do well in this major?

At what stage of my college career do I have to declare this major?

Is it competitive to get accepted into the department?

What grade point average is required?

Where are most of the classes in this major held on campus?

Is it possible for me to sit in on a class?

What skills will I have upon completion of this major?

How long has this been a major on this campus?

Is there any possibility of this major being eliminated or merged with another discipline in the near future?

Is the school sensitive to language barriers on the part of its teaching assistants?

Are the teaching assistants evaluated on their teaching skills by the faculty?

How much access will I have to full faculty members?

What is a typical course of study each year in this major?

Having a set of questions prepared before your appointment with a faculty member will keep you organized during the interview. Faculty members sit through dozens of such interviews each year and appreciate the student who has questions ready. Often, the discussion will veer off into other areas of interest, but at least you will have a solid foundation of questions answered when you leave.

A junior or senior who has personally experienced life on campus can provide you with good answers to some of the questions above. It's best to get answers from both faculty and students in order to get a complete picture of what a major will mean at this school.

If you are one of the many students who is looking at schools and don't have a particular major in mind yet, these are the questions you should be asking:

When do I have to declare a major?
Does each department have a grade point average requirement?

The Campus Bookstore

Campus bookstores contain a wealth of information. Browsing through the stacks of books will provide you with a snapshot of the courses in your major. The books are divided alphabetically into subject areas with all the books required for each course grouped together. Some courses have no books because the instructor prefers to use course packets of copied articles bound together. Other courses have materials provided online.

The books in the bookstore will give you clues to many aspects of the course, such as degree of complexity, amount of reading required, and your own familiarity with the material. And, of course, watch out for "sticker shock." College books are very expensive today, and undergraduates have huge book bills each semester. Parents urge students to buy used books, but, because of the information explosion, many books become out of date very quickly, and the instructor opts for the latest edition.

Volunteering

Offering to work without pay can open doors for your future. Many places that do exciting work will gladly accept your services for free. In return, you have a chance to see how the organization works and determine whether it's a place you'd like to spend your career. Formerly, the only place young people could work was pushing a book cart around a hospital corridor. Today, the world of the volunteer has greatly expanded and offers people access to many places of work.

The second advantage of volunteering is that the people you meet may be able to steer you to other opportunities. One student volunteered for the campus-sponsored Habitat for Humanity, the group that helps people build their own homes. While hammering away, she met an editor for a business publication. When a job opened up, he suggested that she submit her résumé, which led to a job after graduation.

Whether it's riding a night ministry bus or conducting tours of a botanical garden, volunteerism teaches you more about the world than you can learn in the classroom. One student who worked on a rape victims' hotline said she never realized before the extent to which women are devalued in society. And, she said, she was left wondering, why they put up with it. The volunteer conducting tours at the botanical garden might become interested in the emerging field of the medicinal possibilities of plants.

Internships

At most schools you start internships after your sophomore year. Working usually 10–15 hours a week during the school year or summer, students gain needed experience in their field before graduation. No longer is a college degree by itself considered sufficient preparation for the world of work. Employers look for experience on applicants' résumés.

Besides working for an organization, many internships require students to submit written material about their experience, either in the form of a journal or as research papers written about the internship. The professor supervising the internship details what should be included in the journal. Typical topics, written about weekly, for instance, include:

- Interaction with other people at the job
- Skills I am developing at the internship
- Observations about conflict management
- Workplace politics

- I like going to my internship because . . .
- On days that I don't feel like going to the internship, it's usually because . . .
- Suggestions I could make to improve the functioning of my unit
- What I have observed about team dynamics
- Traits of people who are effective at work
- Traits of people who are ineffective at work
- If I were supervising interns, I'd . . .

Research papers about the internship might include:

- An analysis of the audience or clients of the organization
- Interview with someone other than the intern's supervisor who can give an overall view of the goals and plans of the organization
- Short report on the culture (innovations, status quo, team loyalty, and so on) of the organization, featuring what is valued there
- Status report on the work of the intern's unit
- Long report on the relationship of the organization to its competition

Students may earn college credit for completing an internship. Some internships are paid, and others offer only a stipend for travel expenses.

Another type of experiential learning is the cooperative education experience, or co-op. Names such as internship and co-op have become intermingled, but generally co-op jobs are paid. However, students may not receive college credit for co-op jobs.

Katherine Nelson, an English major, worked as a public relations intern for Ameritech Cellular Services for two summers. Then she was hired to work each Friday during the school year. Here are some of the comments she wrote in her internship journal:

> My first summer at Ameritech was great, but this past summer was even better. Some of the projects I worked on included: writing press releases, organizing employee off-site meetings, participating in Ameritech's Internet Task Force, editing the customer newsletter, and other vital PR activities. Out of all of these my favorite task was working on the redesign of Ameritech's Internet site.

I was in charge of getting all the press releases on the site. I also had to make sure each and every product name had been trademarked on our site. For this I had to work with the legal department of Ameritech Corporation. That took a lot of patience.

I spent some time working with the trademark attorney for Ameritech Corporation. I never knew it took so long to trademark and make sure something was legally correct. I'm just glad it's done. Then I moved on to looking at some customer letters. This week I just organized them: I didn't have time to start writing form letters. There are so many things I want to get done and that need to be done. I want to write form letters in response to customers who write letters, organize and establish a system for storing old press releases, and finish a new media kit. I continued my work on the media kit today but didn't get much done because binders needed to go out in the evening mail. So I had to put everything down and help in the crisis.

The company president strongly believes in teamwork. I think this notion of teamwork helps the environment of the office. It builds relationships not just based on work but also on friendship. As I mentioned in class one day, associates go out all the time after work to bars, or they work out together in the Wellness Center

I didn't go into work this Friday because I'm loaded with papers to do for the end of the semester. I hate telling them I can't come in; I feel they might think I don't care or that I don't have any type of responsibility. But, if I don't graduate, I won't be able to get a job anywhere. I haven't spent my parents' money to go to work behind a cash register. Like my mom said, they have to understand that you are still in school and that it is your number one priority. I just hope they realize that.

I have to commend Ameritech for its excellent internship program. They treat the interns royally. This past summer there were 17 of us, most of us from UIC. We had an orientation day, two lunches with the president of the company, a tour of a cellular tower site, and a final event, which was both fun and painful.

We played Whirlybird. The basics of the game were you sit in a bumper car and you wear a mitt. The object is for your team to get the ball into the basket. I walked away with two huge bruises on my legs, but overall it was a lot of fun. Afterwards we had lunch in a restaurant by the office where each intern received a plaque and a whole duffel bag of Ameritech brand goodies.

My dream would be to continue working at Ameritech Cellular as a full-time employee or as an associate.

Contacting Professional Associations

Many professions have associations that keep their members informed of the latest trends affecting their jobs and also to give young people who are thinking of joining this profession information about what the jobs involve. There is a list of professional associations in the appendix of this book. You can look up on the Internet the Web page for the associations you are interested in to learn more. Most of those you contact will provide you with brochures and fact sheets about the profession. You also should ask about upcoming seminars in your city sponsored by the association, another great way to network with people who are already in your field of interest.

Your Part-Time Job

Deciding on a major involves talking to experts, hearing advice, keeping notes, and reading about occupations. Think of all this work as your part-time job; going to school is your full-time job. Every day check off a few more tasks so that you don't become overwhelmed with the whole process—a phone call to set up an information interview, a quick stop at the college counseling office. Just do a little every day.

CHAPTER 5

DESCRIPTIONS OF MAJORS

Majors mean much more than their names imply. While "geography" may sound like looking at a globe and memorizing the names of nations, today it includes the study of terrain and natural resources as well as the implications for ownership of these resources. It also requires that students develop skills in map reading and design and aerial photo interpretation.

As you will see when you read the college course listings online, some colleges go to great lengths to describe what a major means at their school; others merely list what the requirements for a particular major are. Listed below are descriptions of majors as written by the colleges noted. This list will give you an idea of what you can expect when you study a particular major. Philosophies and approaches will vary from school to school. This is a good chapter to read if you have no idea of what your major will be. It's also a good source for broadening your understanding of majors. You might find one here to investigate further.

Anthropology
Beloit College
Beloit, WI

Anthropology is the study of human cultural diversity as it has developed over time and through space, as well as in relation to biology and the environment. The aim of the program is to provide students a strong foundation in the main sub-fields of anthropology—including cultural anthropology (the study of contemporary cultures and social organization), archaeology (the study of cultures and social organization of the past), physical anthropology (human biological diversity, both in comparative perspective and as it has developed over time), and anthropological linguistics (the relationship of language to culture and social organization). Advanced courses as well as independent research allow majors to focus their studies in preparation for a wide range of careers, both in anthropology itself as well as in other professional fields, including international education, law, medicine, social work, public health, urban planning, forensics, and cultural resource management.

Art
Grinnell College
Grinnell, IA

The Department of Art provides curricular opportunities for the development of technical skills, aesthetic judgment, and historical understanding. Participation in both studio and art-history courses stimulates critical thinking and refines creative potentials in the visual arts. The Permanent Collection of original works of art especially works on paper in the Print and Drawing Study Room, supplements formal course study.

Art Therapy
Whittier College
Whittier, CA

Art Therapy is a human service profession that utilizes art media, images, the creative art process and patient/client responses to the created products as reflections of an individual's development, abilities, personality, interests, concerns and conflicts. Art Therapy practice is based on knowledge of human developmental and psychological theories which are implemented in the full spectrum of models of assessment and treatment including educational, psychodynamic, cognitive, transpersonal and other therapeutic means of reconciling emotional conflicts, fostering self-awareness, developing social skills, managing behavior, solving problems, reducing anxiety, aiding reality orientation and increasing self-esteem.

Art Therapy is an effective treatment for the developmentally, medically, educationally, socially, or psychologically impaired; and is practiced in mental health, rehabilitation, medical, educational, and forensic institutions. Populations of all ages, races, and ethnic backgrounds are served by art therapists in individual, couples, family, and group therapy formats.

Educational, professional and ethical standards for art therapists are regulated by The American Art Therapy Association, Inc. The Art Therapy Credentials Board, an independent organization, grants post-graduate supervised experience. The Registered Art Therapist who successfully completes the written examination administered by the Art Therapy Credentials Board is qualified as Board Certified (A.T.R.-BC), a credential requiring maintenance through Continuing Education credits.

Biology
California Institute of Technology
Pasadena, CA

Recent dramatic progress in our understanding of the nature of life has revolutionized the science of biology. Applications of the methods, concepts, and approaches of modern mathematics, physics, chemistry, and information science are providing deep insight into basic biological problems such as the manner in which genes and viruses replicate themselves; the control of gene expression in cells; the regulation of cellular activity; the mechanisms of growth and development; and the nature and interactions of nerve activity, brain function, and behavior. Qualified experimental and computational biologists will find opportunities for challenging work in basic research as well as in medicine and in biotechnology.

Business Administration
Elmhurst College
Elmhurst, IL

The Center for Business and Economics is dedicated to preparing its students for successful careers in a global economy characterized by complex issues, ambiguity and change. A key belief underlying the Center's programs is that success in business generally depends on: specialized skills; awareness and understanding beyond a field of specialization; and such personal attributes as leadership skills, adaptability, healthy self-esteem, competency in problem solving and the ability to communicate effectively. The Center affords the opportunity for each student to develop these skills, perspectives and personal attributes, recognizing that students come to the program with differing needs and expectations.

Chemistry
University of Connecticut
Storrs, CT

Members of the Department engage in extensive research programs in the areas of experimental and theoretical analytical, biological, inorganic, organic, physical and polymer chemistry. Research activities involve the synthesis and characterization of new solid state materials, development of new analytical methods, including methods for separations and purification, characterization of new and known materials by spectroscopic and other physical methods, synthesis and applications of new materials in catalysis and related areas, and chemistry and photochemistry of organic and bioorganic materials.

Classics
Syracuse University
Syracuse, NY

The study of classics focuses on stimulating and important concepts that, originally defined and refined by classical authors, lead to an increased awareness of the complexities of a nation's culture, its institutions, and its underlying values. Freedom, justice, absolute and relative moral values, and the role of the individual in society are still issues of great concern today and are the touchstones by which we measure the accomplishments of civilization. Students of the classics analyze these and other themes of classical literature in the context of their continuing intellectual and emotional influence on Western civilization and the modern world. To this end, students of the classics study the languages of ancient Greece and Rome. Beginning, intermediate, and advanced courses in such authors as Homer, Sophocles, Plato, Cicero, Virgil, and Augustine provide students with the opportunity to examine the contributions of these seminal thinkers to the intellectual traditions of the Western world.

Communication and Theatre
DePauw University
Greencastle, IN

Students in communication and theatre study the process by which messages are devised and disseminated. Attention is given to the various roles and stages in the communication process. The contexts of communication, from interpersonal communication to mass communication, are analyzed and distinguished. As a crossroads discipline, communication is studied from both the humanities and social science perspectives. The study of communication is built around a framework that allows for an understanding of theory, opportunity for criticism of messages and practice and research in the discipline.

Students will study a wide range of communication areas, including speech communication and rhetoric, interpersonal communication, mass communication, theatre and voice science.

Communication students can apply their understanding of this vital process in a variety of fields, such as corporate communication, public relations, personnel, advertising, marketing, law, mass media, sales, public service and the performing arts.

Computer Science
Mount Holyoke College
South Hadley, MA

The Computer Science Program is designed to meet the broad needs of students in a liberal arts environment. Computer science students learn to write programs well, but the fundamental objective of the program is to provide a broader perspective: the science of computing. The focus of the computer science program is to investigate the power, the limitations, and the applications of computing. The current computer science offerings are designed to meet the needs of students whose fields of interest include the following:

- Computer Science

The computer science major offers a solid preparation for graduate school. As part of their studies, students interested in this track usually work on a project for one and one-half to two years and write a thesis. They should also acquire a strong theoretical founding by studying the theory of algorithms and computation.

- Philosophy and Psychology

The field of computer science investigates many of the same questions found in these sister fields, but from a different perspective. Students of the philosophy of the mind or psychology can sharpen their arguments by including artificial intelligence and computer vision in their curriculum.

• Economics, Management, Mathematics and the Sciences

As computers continue to make their way into our everyday lives, managers should have a working knowledge of computer science to make quality decisions about how to use computers in their operations. Economists, mathematicians, and scientists are increasingly using computers as a modeling tool in their research. There is great potential for interdisciplinary research collaboration between computer scientists and colleagues from other disciplines.

Criminal Justice
The University of Illinois at Chicago
Chicago, IL

Criminal Justice is a social and behavioral science field of study that selects crime, law, and the criminal justice system for its subject matter. Using social science methodologies, the program examines the nature, extent, and causes of crime in various settings, the impact of crime on victims and society, and both formal and informal responses to crime. These responses include individual and community reactions, the investigation of crimes and arrest of offenders by the police, and their prosecution, defense, and adjudication by the courts; and an array of sentencing and correctional outcomes. The nature and effectiveness of criminal justice reform efforts are also studied.

The degree prepares graduates for a broad range of professional roles in the criminal justice system, as well as the broader legal system. It also serves as entry to graduate programs of criminal justice and related research and professional programs such as law, sociology, public administration, paralegal studies and various social services.

Economics
University of Wisconsin, Madison
Madison, WI

A major in economics gives students a greater understanding of how people, businesses, and governments respond to their economic environment. Many of the issues that fill the newspapers—jobs, wages, taxes, the cost of living, inequality, pollution, poverty, and economic growth—are, in fundamental ways, economic issues. The daily decisions of businesses and consumers are largely economic. Economists seek to understand the decisions of businesses, consumers, and current economic issues by developing a systematic and thorough understanding of precisely how the economic system operates, including the mechanisms by which resources are allocated, prices determined, income redistributed, and economic growth promoted.

The analytical method of economics recognizes that various choices are open to a society in solving its economic problems. Students are often attracted to economics as a discipline precisely because they want to understand the decisions of people and businesses and to better understand and evaluate economic policy. To begin to approach these issues as an economist requires an understanding of economic theory, empirical methodology, and an understanding of the institutional details and advanced practice gained from intensive study of specific subfields of economics. Consequently, the undergraduate economics major is organized around a progression of courses that first provides a broad introduction to economics, then develops the theoretical tools that provide the foundation of modern economic thought, and finishes with advanced courses designed to provide greater in-depth knowledge of specific fields (such as labor markets, industrial organization, international economics, public finance, banking and finance, macroeconomics, microeconomics, and econometrics).

An economics major is valuable in the job market because the major is designed to train people to think analytically and clearly about a wide variety of issues. Many employers value this skill. An economics major is also good preparation for graduate work in a number of areas: Business, law, public policy, economics, public planning, and environmental studies.

Education
Macalester College
Saint Paul, MN

Curricular offerings provide a vibrant and challenging environment for students, faculty and staff to pursue a wide range of interests including both public school teaching and teaching in contexts that do not require state licensing (e.g., teaching abroad, private school positions, artists-in-residence, youth development and other outreach programs, etc.) Opportunities are also provided to pursue varied dimensions of educational studies addressing pressing societal issues on local, national, and international levels (e.g., urban education, educational policy, multicultural and anti-bias-education, environmental education, civic education, youth development, international education, and education-centered responses to social justice and reform imperatives).

The curriculum is centered in four mutually supportive themes:

Social Advocacy: John Dewey stated, "Education is the fundamental method of social progress and reform." These words assume special significance at a time when there is widespread recognition that current social and educational policies and practices designed to fulfill the needs and aspirations of children and youth are in crisis. In response, the curriculum is designed to promote social responsibility (including preparation for social service and social leadership) and cultural pluralism (including concern for gender, race, class, international, and urban issues), especially as these commitments contribute to the advancement of social, political, and educational welfare of children and youth.

Life Span Development: In order to address the needs and aspirations of children and youth, the curriculum reflects current theory and research, which articulates a developmental continuum of human learning, growth, change, crisis and renewal. The study of human development is conducted in an inclusive and integrative manner, addressing patterns and processes across the domains of cognitive, affective, intuitive, social, physical, and moral growth, and throughout the age continuum from early childhood through young adulthood. The educational implications of individual variations in intellectual, emotional, and physical capabilities and factors related to gender, class, race, or cultural heritage are also addressed. Additionally, the interplay among developmental processes on personal, organizational, and societal levels is carefully considered.

Diversity: The curriculum further reflects commitment to the concept of human diversity as a *resource* to schools and society. It is assumed that both special challenges and unique opportunities are associated with individual variations in intellectual, emotional, and physical capabilities and factors related to gender, class, race, and cultural heritage. Students are expected to assess implications of their own cultural heritage, to grow in understanding and compassion as they explore the perspectives of others, and to act upon their growing awareness in supportive and life-enhancing ways.

Civic Engagement: The curriculum is further designed to ensure ongoing and developmentally appropriate opportunities for application, integration, and evaluation of educational theory and practice. In doing so the curriculum promotes understanding of development-in-context, thereby acknowledging the dynamic and complex constellation of factors and relationships that contribute to the educational process. A developmental sequence of field experience is integrated throughout education course work beginning with opportunities to develop observational skills, then to participate in activities that support instruction, and finally, to assume instructional roles. Each student's fieldwork is structured to ensure opportunities to interact with students across the age spectrum from early childhood through adolescence before selecting an age for specialization. Field experiences are further structured to include experiences with exceptional students and work in pluralistic educational settings.

Engineering
Purdue University
West Lafayette, IN

Engineering is a professional field that influences almost every element of our society. Perhaps no other profession is more truly concerned with the safety of health and property. The goals of the engineering profession—maintenance of high ethical standards and quality performance—are integral to the academic programs in all Schools of Engineering.

A student is expected to graduate with a solid technical background that will enable him or her to take a positive place in society and contribute to finding solutions to the complex problems facing our nation.

English
St. Cloud State University
St. Cloud, MN

Students entering courses in the English Department will find opportunities in literary studies; rhetorical studies; linguistics; pedagogical studies, including Teaching English as a Second Language (TESL); cultural, cross-cultural, and historical studies of literature and language; theoretical perspectives on literature and language; and practical applications of language in professional, business, and political environments. In each of these diverse areas of study, students will come to a greater understanding of the crucial role of language in constructing meaning, building community, negotiating social, political, and economic goals, and clarifying and articulating ethical and aesthetic values—and, indeed, attempting to glimpse the spiritual meaning of human experience.

The English Department is not only multidisciplinary within its own walls; faculty in the department have strong teaching and other professional collaborations with colleagues in other departments, and students are encouraged to gain cross-disciplinary experience and perspectives as well, through minors, second majors, or other thoughtfully selected course work. English students are also encouraged to experiment with applications of their coursework in venues outside the classroom through internships and volunteer positions.

In local, regional, and national surveys, employers continually rank communication skills at the top when asked to list job qualifications. Sensitivity for subtle nuance in language, skill in reading text, people, and relationships, appreciation of ambiguity, and creative and critical habits of thought are the hallmarks of a good English student. These are exactly the vocational skills for the information economy of the Twenty-First Century. Hence, well-prepared English majors and minors can expect to be successful in careers across the entire range of the economy as long as they also have the specific technical qualifications required.

Environmental Sciences
University of Massachusetts
Amherst, MA

Students learn how to meet the challenges of creating a safe and healthy environment and how to recognize and control the impact of pollution and environmental stress on ecosystems. Faculty and students seek practical solutions to complex environmental problems by crossing traditional disciplinary boundaries. Students learn how to integrate and apply knowledge from the appropriate areas of basic science, economics, and policy. Environmental Sciences faculty and students address problems caused by ecosystem degradation from physical alteration of the environment and chemical contaminants from industrial activities, agriculture, food production, and inadequate resource management.

French
University of Colorado
Boulder, CO

Beyond providing mastery of the language skills (listening, speaking, reading, writing) of modern French needed for all purposes of daily life, the major introduces students to a central tradition of western and indeed world culture. Since the Middle Ages, French literature, thought, taste, and art have helped shape the essential experience and self-understanding of humanity at large. Survey courses and upper-division seminars offer a range of exposures to the French cultural past and the far-flung ethnic and national diversity of the French-speaking present, exploring such distinctively French contributions to world culture as: Arthurian romance, troubador poetry, and Gothic architecture; the love sonnets of the Pleiade, the comic novels of Rabelais, and the essays of Montaigne; the neoclassical theatre of Corneille, Moliere, and Racine and the critical philosophy of Descartes and Pascal; the Enlightenment philosophies of Voltaire, Diderot, and Rousseau; the psychological refinements of French fiction from Mme de La Fayette to Proust; artistic revolutions like impressionism and surrealism; the renewal of artistic conventions in the Theatre of the Absurd, the New Novel, and the cinema of the New Wave; the French-language literature of Africa, Canada, and the Caribbean; and the vital presence of French writers in major movements of twentieth-century thought like existentialism, structuralism, feminism, psychoanalysis, and contemporary cultural studies and multiculturalism.

In pursuing an undergraduate degree in French, majors are expected to acquire the following forms of knowledge:

- an awareness of the fundamental outlines of the history of French literature from the Middle Ages to the present;
- familiarity with significant works of French literature and awareness of the literary culture of the French-speaking world;
- awareness of the historical context in which particular works were written and of the relation between literature and other forms of cultural expression (e.g., art, philosophy, politics, religion);
- awareness of contemporary French culture, politics, and current events;
- awareness of a range of literary genres, their development and reception, as well as relevant critical methodologies;
- and understanding of the grammatical structure of modern standard French.

In addition, students completing the degree in French are expected to acquire:

- the ability to speak and understand modern, spoken standard French sufficient for all purposes of daily life and for intellectual discussion in academic settings;
- the ability to read and write modern standard French with sufficient fluency and correctness for successful literary or linguistic analysis of French texts;
- the ability to analyze and interpret literary texts in terms of style, plot, structure, characters, themes, and the use of literary devices;
- the ability to communicate such analyses and interpretations simply in French or at a more sophisticated level in English, and to discuss a wide range of topics concerning French culture, civilization, and current events; and
- the ability to follow with reasonable comprehension authentic French broadcasts or film.

Geography
The University of Montana
Missoula, MT

Geography provides a broad-ranging perspective on humans as inhabitants and transformers of the face of the earth. The search for this understanding involves thorough study of the physical earth, its habitation by humans, and the resulting diversity of regions and places. Geographers study the physical earth by examining the interlocking systems of the natural environment including climate, landforms, soils, and biota. Humans are studied by examining those diverse historical, cultural, social, economic, and political structures and processes that affect the location and spatial organization of population groups and their activities. Regions and places, whether described as nations, cities, ecological units or landscapes, are studied by integrating and interpreting their physical and human relationships in an effort to better understand them and the problems they face.

Geographers are often found working in business, industry, government, planning, and teaching. Their tasks may range from determining the optimal location for a new supermarket to doing the biophysical and socioeconomic studies required for urban and regional planning. Geographers trained in cartography may find professional opportunities in the various aspects of making and communicating with maps.

The Department of Geography maintains particular strengths in each of the following major branches within the discipline:

1. geography and society (geography of towns and settlements, economic geography, and migration and population change);
2. physical geography (biogeography, paleo-environments, climate and global change;
3. human B environment interaction (environmental rehabilitation, water policy, and environmental hazards);
4. regional geography (with particular strengths in the geography of Central Asia and the Caspian Basin, but also North America, Africa, South Asia and Europe);
5. geographic techniques (cartography and GIS, field methods, quantitative and qualitative methods, and palynology).

Geology
Colgate University
Hamilton, NY

Geology is the study of the physical and chemical nature of the Earth, the evolution and impact of life on the planet and the global processes active both now and in the past. An understanding of geology is developed through the scientific study of fossils, sedimentary, igneous and metamorphic rocks, and past and present-day ecosystems, including the oceanic realm.

Introductory courses are designed to contribute significantly to a liberal arts education and an understanding of the environment. Advanced courses provide the highest possible level of general and professional training for concentrators.

A concentration in geology provides students with the opportunity to pursue careers in the geological and environmental sciences, business and education, as well as government and public service. Upon graduation, many geology majors go on to graduate study in geology, hydrology, oceanography, environmental sciences, and environmental policy and law. Other graduates go directly into a wide spectrum of employment situations, including business, environmental consulting, teaching and administration in schools and museums, and mining and petroleum-related jobs.

Kinesiology
University of Maryland at College Park
College Park, MD

This program offers students the opportunity to study the interdisciplinary body of knowledge related to human physical activity and sport and to pursue specific specializations so that each individual can prepare for a particular career goal within the broad discipline. There is no intent to orient all students toward a particular specialized interest, orientation or career. However, many current students are pursuing careers in medically related fields (i.e., physical therapy, physician, chiropractory), in the fitness industry (i.e., corporate fitness, personal training, health fitness director) as well as in the sport industry (sport management, sport marketing, events management, equipment sales, athletic director). The program provides a hierarchical approach to the study of human movement. First, a broad core of knowledge is recognized as being necessary foundations to advanced and more specific courses. Secondly, at the "Options" level, students select from approved upper level KNES courses which they believe will provide the knowledge to pursue whatever future goal they set for themselves. To further strengthen specific areas of interest, students should carefully select electives. The program culminates with a senior seminar class in which students write a substantial paper and discuss the implications of research.

The curriculum offers students the opportunity to study the body of knowledge of human movement and sport, and to choose specific programs of study that allow them to pursue a particular goal related to the discipline. There is no intent to orient all students toward a particular specialized interest or occupation. This program provides a hierarchical approach to the study of human movement. First, a core of knowledge is recognized as being necessary for all students in the curriculum. These core courses are considered foundational to advanced and more specific courses. Secondly, at the "options" level, students may select from two sets of courses that they believe will provide the knowledge to pursue whatever goal they set for themselves in the future. To further strengthen specific areas of interest, students should carefully select related studies, courses and electives.

Mathematics
The University of Michigan
Ann Arbor, MI

Mathematics is sometimes called the Queen of the Sciences; because of its unforgiving insistence on accuracy and rigor, it is a model for all of science. It is a field that serves science but also stands on its own as one of the greatest edifices of human thought. Much more than a collection of calculations, it is finally a system for the analysis of form.

Alone among the sciences, it is a discipline where almost every fact can and must be proved.

The study of mathematics is an excellent preparation for many careers; the patterns of careful logical reasoning and analytical problem solving essential to mathematics are also applicable in contexts where quantity and measurement play only minor roles. Thus students of mathematics may go on to excel in medicine, law, politics, or business as well as any of a vast range of scientific careers. Special programs are offered for those interested in teaching mathematics at the elementary or high school level or in actuarial mathematics, the mathematics of insurance.

The other programs split between those that emphasize mathematics as an independent discipline and those that favor the application of mathematical tools to problems in other fields. There is considerable overlap here and any of these programs may serve as preparation for either further study in a variety of academic disciplines, including mathematics itself, or intellectually challenging careers in a wide variety of corporate and governmental settings.

Medical Technology
The University of Kansas
Lawrence, Kansas

The clinical laboratory scientist (medical technologist) performs laboratory analyses on blood, tissue, and fluids in the human body using precision instruments such as microscopes and automatic analyzers. Test results play an important role in the detection, diagnosis, and treatment of disease. Medical technologists establish and monitor quality control programs and design or modify procedures to assure accurate results. They recognize interdependency of tests and understand physiological conditions affecting test results in order to provide data used by a physician in determining the presence, extent, and as far as possible, the cause of disease.

Music
Duke University
Durham, NC

The music major may be considered a component of one's general education—a central focus of an otherwise diverse experience—or it may be treated as a pre-professional program. The two views are certainly not mutually exclusive: the choice of this major need not imply any specific vocational commitment. In practice, the music major can provide either a general survey of music as a liberal arts experience or as a path into various areas of specialization. The music department cuts a wide swath across the fields of music. In keeping with its goal of musical excellence within the liberal arts environment, the music department has attracted a versatile faculty of distinguished performers, conductors, composers, and scholars.

What happens to students after they leave the music department? Many graduates have continued their academic and professional studies at universities and professional institutions in this country and abroad. Many enjoy active careers as college teachers, private teachers, classical and jazz performers, musicologists, composers, conductors, and opera or concert managers. Others have held posts such as the first professional president of the New York Philharmonic, the chair of the National Endowment for the Arts, the artistic director for a large recording company, and as arranger-conductor for Hollywood TV productions. Our graduates have won the BMI Young Composer Awards, the ASCAP Foundation's Grants to Young Composers, and the Charles Ives Fellowship from American Academy of Arts and Letters. Thus, the professional relevance of a major in music seems to encompass a wide range of careers. Many students have chosen not to pursue music as a career, but have nonetheless found the music major to be an excellent focus of their liberal arts education, preparing them for graduate and professional study in fields such as law, medicine, or business.

Courses include many kinds of instruction: applied lessons, history and theory lectures and seminars, harmony classes, composition seminars, ensemble participation, practical laboratory work (such as ear-training), coaching sessions for conductors and chamber musicians, and jazz improvisation. Emphasis is placed equally on theory and practice, and students' musical activity can vary widely across the spectrum from composing their own music to endeavoring to understand the technical, historical, and sociological context of other composers' music.

Nursing
The University of Iowa
Iowa City, IA

The Bachelor of Science in Nursing (B.S.N.) is designed to provide preparation for careers in the hospital care of patients and in community agencies such as public health services, schools, homes, and industries. It also serves as the base for graduate study in nursing.

In addition to the advantages of combining general education with specialized career preparation, a college or university program offers the advantages of full participation in the social, cultural, and recreational activities of a highly diverse campus community. In nursing, no less than in other pursuits, a college or university background enables people not only to be prepared for a career but to be able to achieve a life of thought and action informed by knowledge, introspection, and contemplation.

The program prepares professional nurses to be primary health care providers who are able to engage in a broad range of health promotion and teaching activities and to coordinate care in any sector of the health care system.

The nursing major provides a basis for nurses' roles in wellness and health promotion, in acute care, and in long-term care for chronic illness. The professional nurse provides care to individuals, families, groups, and communities along a continuum of health, illness, and disability.

In addition to providing care, the nurse serves as a coordinator of health care by organizing and facilitating the delivery of comprehensive, efficient, and appropriate service to individuals, families, groups, and communities. The nurse demonstrates the ability to conceptualize the total continuing health needs of the patient, including legal and ethical aspects of care. The program's goal is to produce graduates who are competent, committed, creative, and compassionate.

Occupational Therapy
University of New Hampshire
Durham, NH

Occupational therapy enables people to participate in daily life activities including leisure, work, self-care, and home management. Occupational therapists work with people of all ages to gain or regain skills and abilities or adapt tasks within their natural environment. Occupational therapy education includes studies in liberal arts, biological, behavioral, and health sciences, and occupational science and occupational therapy or restoring individual capacity for functional independence and adaptation in the context of clients' environments.

The occupational therapy program includes studies in three major areas: 1) liberal arts; 2) biological, behavioral, and health sciences;

and 3) occupational therapy theory and practice. Observation and guided practice in local clinical sites are an integral part of some courses. Following completion of the four-year academic program, students are placed in three 3-month, full-time fieldwork experiences.

Philosophy
Amherst College
Amherst, MA

An education in philosophy conveys a sense of wonder about our world and ourselves. It achieves this partly through exploration of philosophical texts, which comprise some of the most stimulating creations of the human intellect, and partly through direct and personal engagement with philosophical issues. At the same time, an education in philosophy cultivates a critical stance to this elicited puzzlement, which would otherwise merely bewilder us.

The central topics of philosophy include the nature of reality (metaphysics); the ways we represent reality to ourselves and to others (philosophy of mind and philosophy of language); the nature and analysis of inference and reasoning (logic); knowledge and the ways to acquire it (epistemology and philosophy of science); and value and morality (aesthetics, ethics, and political philosophy). Students who major in philosophy are encouraged to study broadly in all of these areas of philosophy.

Physics
Northeastern University
Boston, MA

Physics examines the fundamental principles that govern natural phenomena, ranging in scale from collisions of subatomic particles, through the behavior of solids, liquids, and biomolecules, to exploding stars and colliding galaxies.

The program aims to help students experience the intellectual stimulation of studying physics and astrophysics and the excitement of front-line research; understand the basic principles and techniques of physics-related careers; and prepare for graduate study in physics or related fields.

The department offers four levels of undergraduate courses: descriptive courses for non-science majors with limited mathematical background; general survey courses for students in scientific and engineering fields; advanced courses primarily intended for physics majors; and highly advanced courses primarily intended for prospective graduate students.

In addition to work in industrial, government, or high-technology laboratories in areas of applied physics, students may find opportunities in such fields as biological physics, computer science, geophysics, medical and radiation physics, and engineering. Many physics majors pursue advanced degrees in physics and related fields.

Political Science
Idaho State University
Pocatello, ID

The study of governments and human beings as decision makers is at once an ancient discipline and one of the most recently developed social sciences. Political inquiry reaches back to the recorded beginnings of human society, for individuals have always been curious about the nature of governments, the bases of authority and personality of leaders, the obligations of followers, and consequences of public policies. Although interest persists in these matters, inquiry has broadened to include scientific observations about politics that utilize relatively new techniques of analysis that are common to many of the social sciences.

The newer emphasis is upon systematic procedures of investigation, rigorous standards of proof, comparative analysis and interdisciplinary studies.

Both of these approaches—the traditional and the behavioral—are offered in the undergraduate and graduate levels of study. The curriculum provides background in the theory and practice of politics and techniques of methodological inquiry for the student with general interests. It offers training of a general and specific nature that is useful for persons planning to seek careers in education, the legal profession, state and local government, urban and regional planning, the federal bureaucracy and journalism, or in any of the proliferating quasi-public organizations that seek to monitor the political processes or to influence the content of public policy.

Psychology
University of Notre Dame
South Bend, IN

Psychology is the scientific study of the behavior of organisms with a primary focus on human behavior. It is concerned with the biological and environmental determinants of behavior as reflected in the study of physiological, sensory, perceptual, cognitive, motivational, learning, developmental, aging and social processes. The undergraduate program seeks a balance between exposure to basic psychological principles and theories and their extension to the applied areas such as child education, counseling, mental retardation and behavioral deviancy.

Religious Studies
University of Colorado
Boulder, CO

The curriculum in Religious Studies includes the study of traditions such as Buddhism, Hinduism, Taosim, Confucianism, Judaism, Islam, Christianity, and Native American and other traditional religious, and topics such as ritual studies, peace studies, religion and literature, women and religion, and religion and psychology.

The undergraduate degree in religious studies emphasizes knowledge and awareness of:

• the beliefs, practices, and institutions of Asian, Western, and Native American/traditional religious traditions;
• one major religious tradition in-depth; and
• different theoretical and methodological approaches to the study of religion.

In addition, students with a degree in religious studies are expected to acquire the ability and skills to:

• identify textual, performative, and artifactual data relevant to the study of religion;
• draw connections between different historical and/or cultural contexts of religion; and
• communicate data analysis and interpretation competently in written form.

Students in this curriculum are expected to gain knowledge of one major religious tradition and identify textual and artifactual data relevant to the study of religion. Central is the ability to draw connections between different historical and/or cultural contexts of religion.

Social Work
University of Illinois at Chicago
Chicago, IL

Social work assists people in the prevention and resolution of social problems. It provides services to those who seek to resolve personal difficulties, and it helps communities organize services to contribute to the well being of all citizens. It plays a significant role in the planning and administration of human service programs and the development of public policy.

Qualified social workers are in demand in every area of professional practice. For example, they are needed to work with children and adults who are mentally ill, emotionally disturbed, delinquent, physically ill, mentally or physically challenged, or economically deprived. Social work is practiced in such settings as social welfare centers, psychiatric and general hospitals, service centers for the aged, and community-based agencies of various types.

The Jane Addams College of Social Work responds to the challenges facing urban America by preparing social work practitioners, scholars, and leaders with a firm grounding in public and private sector issues facing vulnerable populations. The mission of the Jane Addams College of Social Work is to educate professional social workers, develop knowledge, and provide leadership in the development and implementation of policies and services on behalf of the poor, the oppressed, racial and ethnic minorities, and other at-risk urban populations.

Sociology
University of Massachusetts Amherst
Amherst, MA

Sociology studies virtually every aspect of human society: the family, gender, race and ethnic relations, aging, education, work, population, and many others. Its principle goal as a discipline is to understand the workings of human society and to explain social behavior. Although sociologists do study what are commonly regarded as social problems—crime, drug addiction, and poverty, for example—they also examine fundamental social processes present in any society: social change, conflict, and inequality. Sociology is less concerned with finding practical solutions to social problems than with achieving a fundamental understanding of the social world.

The Sociology major provides the foundation of a broad liberal education, but it also prepares students to undertake rewarding careers. In addition to graduate work in the social sciences, sociology majors go on to graduate study in social work, law, and education, and to careers in business as well as in the human and social service professions and in the criminal justice system. The sociology major does not provide social work or criminal justice training, but it develops knowledge and skills useful for students who will enter careers in those fields.

Theatre
Knox College
Galesburg, IL

The study of theatre and dance helps a student to understand more fully basic human qualities and to improve skills of expression, both emotively and intellectually. The department of theatre and dance is designed to accommodate a wide variety of interests. The department offers courses in the theoretical, literary, and historical concepts of theatre and in practical aspects of theatre production. All are intended to broaden the liberal education of students. For students who like to attend good theatre productions, the department provides exposure to great works from the vast catalogue of past and present drama through an extensive program in the campus theatres.

For students bent on furthering their avocational production skills, the department heartily encourages them to participate in production activities in different capacities and at various levels of expertise. In the past, non-majors have acted, directed, designed, and both chaired and worked on every production crew, according to their desires and talents. Many opportunities are available, and credit can be earned for active participation.

Students who major in theatre fall into two broad categories. Some of them view theatre as a viable route to the personal, creative, and intellectual development needed for whatever career they choose to pursue in the future. Some seek pre-professional training for theatre careers in professional and educational theatre. Many have completed advanced graduate and conservatory work at leading institutions and have careers in theatre and in college, secondary and elementary teaching.

Keep on Searching

Search online or in hard copy catalog course listings for descriptions of the majors that interest you. Browse. Other majors may draw your attention. Compare a major in one catalog with the same major in another one. Every school creates a major differently, combining the school's unique culture, the research of its faculty, and the academic strength of students who have studied there previously. Reading the descriptions will give you a sense of what a particular major means at each school and whether studying that particular major interests you.

CHAPTER 6

COURSES FOR DIFFERENT MAJORS

Mapping out a four-year plan for all the courses you are going to take is nearly impossible. Some courses are offered every term; others only occasionally. The timetable of classes, distributed before registration every term, may bring conflicts in timing between two courses. Electives you had your heart set on may never be available when you have time to take them. You can make a rough sketch, but that's all it is—rough.

Students enjoy enrolling in electives, those courses they take by choice. A very popular elective at the University of California at San Diego, for instance, is gospel choir. Both musically gifted and musically interested students join, 500 strong, for hallelujahs. Music majors may also take this course as one of their required music courses.

Grinders, Weeders, Breezes

Among the required courses, watch out for the "grinders." Almost from the first day you set foot on campus, upperclass students will be warning you about certain courses. Taking them is something akin to war. Surviving is considered an accomplishment.

Another category you will encounter is the "weeders," especially prevalent in the sciences and premed curricula. A professor will stand up the first day in organic chemistry and tell students that only one half the class will pass. "You can't all go to med school; there isn't enough room!" he will bellow to the crestfallen students. Or a creative writing instructor will so intimidate students with her critiques of a short story, that the students will drop the course before they've had a chance to understand and adapt to writing short stories.

Some of the courses will be relatively easy, either because of your natural ability or because you were well prepared for the subject in high school. These are the "breezes." Consider these courses way stations along the trip, a place to catch your breath.

Prerequisites

You will quickly tire of seeing the word "prerequisite." Prerequisites, as the name implies, must be completed before you can move on to the next course. The prerequisite courses always seem to lack luster at the time you are taking them. The upper-level courses are the ones that students value for intellectual challenge. They just want to get the "prewrecks" out of the way.

The Logic of Course Sequences for Majors

College builds skills. When you start out in an introductory course, you become familiar with the terrain and the vocabulary. Vocabulary is essential to communication, and each specialty has its own jargon. Imagine a convention of physics majors taking place in Spokane, Washington. Within a very short period of time, no matter where the students attend school, they would be conversing in their own language. They could quickly relate and conversationally move to the problem solving that goes on in their discipline. Same for music majors, psych majors, and so on.

If you enroll in an introductory Russian course, you will quickly see that the alphabet looks quite different from the Roman. Many people who have never studied Russian assume that this is the most difficult part of the course. It is not. Students must learn the alphabet during the first weekend. Until you have mastered that basic building block, there will be no progress in grammar, sentence structure, or reading the great Russian authors.

Sometimes students try to skip the courses they're required to take before the course they want to take. Somehow, they beat the computer or the college registration process and get in without the required courses. They are at a severe disadvantage. It's similar to a course for which you late registered and missed the first two weeks of class. You start the class in week three. Already you feel lost. You wonder how could they have covered so much in just two short weeks. The acceleration is the result of several reasons. The instructor is fresh and eager to impart knowledge in the first two weeks. She or he is not yet exhausted from grading papers and research. Students feel good, refreshed from an intersession break. They are especially attentive and listen carefully to every point the instructor makes. The books the class is using have already been purchased in the bookstore. The late registrants, on the other hand, find that the bookstore is out of the textbook they need and it won't be in for another two weeks. This is the same dilemma that students face who somehow take a course out of sequence. They haven't done the basic groundwork and usually feel behind.

Course sequencing follows logic and is designed to build skills. Once you have learned the basics in 100-level courses (e.g., Human Relationships 101), you are ready to go on to upper-level courses such as Marriage in the Twentieth Century 202, Lesbian and Gay Relationships 204, and so on. As you move up the ladder, you build confidence in what you have learned and apply it to the next subject in your major.

The Majors

Schools differ in what they require of their majors but in the United States most majors involve similar courses. There are exceptions as majors continue to evolve. The National Alumni Forum, for instance, studied the top 70 U.S. colleges and universities and found that one-third no longer require a course in Shakespeare. English majors at Dartmouth, Amherst, and Georgetown, to name a few, are not required to take a course in Shakespeare. Two-thirds of the colleges still require Shakespeare. You and your cousin may have the same major but take different courses because you're at different colleges. An English major at one college will not involve exactly the same courses at another college.

To give you an idea of what you will be studying in a particular major, a sample of courses in specific majors follows. Courses vary from school to school.

Accounting

Introduction to Financial Accounting
Introduction to Managerial Accounting
Intermediate Financial Accounting
Cost Accounting
Auditing
Federal Income Tax I, II
Business Law I, II
Governmental and Non-Profit Accounting
Accounting Information Systems
International Accounting

African-American Studies

Introduction to African-American Studies
African-American Behavioral Patterns
The African-American Family in the United States
Introduction to African-American Literature I
Precolonial Africa
African-American History to 1877
Africans in Latin America and the Caribbean
African Art
Black Politics in the United States
Studies in African-American Poetry
Theory and Criticism in African-American Literature
African-Americans and the Criminal Justice System

Anthropology

Human Evolution
Folklore
Sex and Gender in World Cultures
Old World Archaeology
Culture and Personality
The First Americans

China and Japan: Society and Culture
Cultural Ecology
Geographic Information Systems
Theory and Method in Archaeology

Architecture

Introduction to Architecture
Structures in Design of Steel and Timber Structures
Building Science: Multi-Story Residential/Office Buildings
Design and Technology
Architectural Study in Europe
Architecture Design Laboratory
Advanced Structural Analysis
Computers in Architecture
Theory of Architecture and Building Analysis
Professional Practice

Art and Design

Drawing I, II
Graphic Design I–VIII
Industrial Design, I, II
Sculpture I, II
Photography, I, II
Introduction to Time-Based Visual Arts
Introduction to Computer Graphics
Color Theory
Typography
Painting I, II
Lithography
Relief Printmaking
Media Explorations
Cinema I, II
Video I, II
Art Education
Computer-Aided Design
Advanced Film/Video/Animation
Electronic Visualization

Art History

Art History
Introduction to Art and Art History
History of Art and Architecture I, II
Theories and Methods in the History of Art and Architecture
History of Landscape Architecture
Twentieth Century Architecture
History of Photography I, II
History of Film I, II
History of Design I, II
Art and Architecture of the Ancient World I, II
American Art to 1945
Contemporary Architecture

Biochemistry

Introductory Physics I, II
Biology of Cells and Organisms
Biology of Populations and Communities
Mendelian and Molecular Genetics
General and Analytical Chemistry I, II
Organic Chemistry I, II
Organic Chemistry Laboratory
Physical Chemstry I, II
Physical Chemistry Laboratory
Biochemistry I, II
Intermediate Inorganic Chemistry

Bioengineering

Introduction to Bioengineering
Senior Design I, II
Pattern Recognition
Biomechanics
Fields and Waves in Biological Materials
Biological Signal Analysis
Real-Time Data Processing
Digital Signal Processing

Biology

Biology of Cells and Organisms
Biology of Populations and Communities
Mendelian and Molecular Genetics and Laboratory
Writing in the Biological Sciences
Cell Biology and Laboratory
Vertebrate Embryology
General Microbiology and Laboratory
Developmental Biology and Laboratory
Cell and Molecular Biology
Ultrastructural Cell Biology
Plant Growth and Development and Laboratory
Biochemistry I, II

Chemical Engineering

Introduction to Thermodynamics
Material and Energy Balances
Chemical Engineering: Thermodynamics
Transport Phenomena I, II, III
Chemical Reaction Engineering
Chemical Process Control
Chemical Engineering Laboratory I, II
Senior Design I, II
Properties of Materials
Fortran Programming for Engineers
Electrical Circuit Analysis

Chemistry

General Chemistry I, II
Organic Chemistry I and Laboratory
Organic Chemistry II and Laboratory
Physical Chemistry I and Laboratory
Physical Chemistry II and Laboratory
Inorganic Chemistry I
Introductory Biochemistry
Analytical Chemistry

Civil Engineering

Statics
Strength of Materials
Structural Analysis
Hydraulics and Hydrology
Environmental Pollution Control
Properties of Materials
Composition and Properties of Concrete
Behavior and Design of Metal Structures
Introduction to Transportation and Traffic Engineering
Design of Reinforced Concrete Structures
Soil Mechanics and Foundation Engineering
Senior Design I, II
Finite Element Analysis I
Fortran Programming for Engineers
Electrical Circuit Analysis

Communication

Effective Public Communication
Communication and Culture
Interpersonal Communication
Media Processes and Effects
Communication Technologies
Communication Analysis
Communication in the Corporate Setting
Group Communication
Communication Research
Organizational Communication Media Field Production
Writing for the Media
Professional Speech Writing
Public Opinion and Public Communication

Criminal Justice

Introduction to the Justice System
Law in Society
Principles of Criminal Law
Criminology
Criminal Justice Organizations

Research Methods I, II
Introduction to the Criminal Courts
Senior Studies in Criminal Justice
Juvenile Justice System
Organized White-Collar Crime in the United States

Economics

Macroeconomics in the World Economy: Theory and Applications
Managerial Economics
Business Conditions Analysis
Comparative Economic Systems
Government and Business
History of Economic Thought
Introduction to Mathematical Economics
Econometrics

Electrical Engineering and Computer Science

Statics and Dynamics
Thermodynamics
Engineering Economy
Fortran Programming for Engineers
Electrical Circuit Analysis
Digital Systems
Circuits and Signal Processing
Communication Engineering
Transmission Lines
Electromagnetic Fields
Electronic Devices and Circuits
Electronic Circuit Design
Computer Organization and Programming
Senior Design I, II

Elementary Education

Policy Foundations
The Educative Process
Literacy and Elementary Education
Introductory Fieldwork in Elementary Education

Reading and Writing through the Elementary Grades
Teaching Elementary School Mathematics and Science
Teaching and Learning for Children of Various Abilities and Cultures
Social Studies and Literature in Elementary Education
Student Teaching in the Elementary Grades
Survey of Characteristics of Exceptional Children

English

Understanding Literature
American Literature and Culture
Introduction to Literary Criticism
History of English Literature I: Beginnings to 1700
History of English Literature II: 1700 to 1900
Topics in Literature: 1900 to the present
Introduction to Nonfiction Writing
Advanced Nonfiction Writing
Introduction to Fiction or Poetry Writing
Advanced Fiction or Poetry Writing
Writing for the Media

Finance

Personal Finance
Introduction to Managerial Finance
Investments
Managerial Finance
Portfolio Management
Security Analysis
Options and Futures Markets
Corporate Financial Strategy
Introduction to Money and Banking
International Finance
Small Business Finance

French

Introduction to French Literature I, II
Conversation and Composition I, II
Writing in the Major

Topics in Twentieth-Century French Literature
French Literature of the Middle Ages
French Civilization I: Medieval and Renaissance
French Civilization II: Seventeenth and Eighteenth Centuries
Oral and Written French
Advanced Oral and Written French
Methods and Principles of Translation

Geology

Principles of Physical Geology
Principles of Historical Geology
Mineralogy
Topics in Modern Geology
Introduction to Petrology
Principles of Sedimentology and Stratigraphy
Introduction to Paleontology
Field Geology
Structural Geology and Tectonics

German

Introduction to German Literature in English Translation
Intermediate German I, II: Reading Emphasis
Advanced German I, II
Writing in the Study of German
Applied Grammar
Structures of German and English
Pronouncing German
German Poetry
German Prose Fiction
Topics in German Literature and Culture
Culture Studies I, II, III

Health Information Management

Introduction to the Health Care System
Medical Science I, II
Health Information Management I, II, III
Technical Affiliation

Legal Aspects of Medical Records
Coding and Classification Systems I, II
Analysis of Health Care Data
Quality Evaluation and Management
Management I, II
Computers in Health Care
Systems Analysis
Introduction to Research
Health Information Research
Current Issues in Health Information Management
Financial Management
Clinical Practicum

History

Western Civilization to 1648
Western Civilization since 1648
American Civilization to the Late Nineteenth Century
American Civilization since the Late Nineteenth Century
World History
Europe: 1815 to 1914
China since 1911
Latin America since 1850
The Middle East since 1258
Military History: War since Napoleon
Senior Seminar: Topics in Research and Writing
Teaching History and the Related Disciplines
Topics in African History
Topics in Revolutionary and Early National United States History

Human Nutrition and Dietetics

Foods
Nutrition
Nutrition Care Planning
Instructional Design
Management
Science of Foods
Food and Its Facets

Science and Nutrition
Nutrition through the Lifecycle
Nutrition through the Lifecycle Practicum
Clinical Nutrition I, II, III
Clinical Practice I, II, III
Quantity Food Production
Quantity Food Production Practicum
Food Service Management
Food Service Management Practicum
The Research Process
Management in Human Nutrition and Medical Dietetics
Professional Practice
Fundamentals of Biochemistry
Principles of Delivering Public Health Nutrition Services
Human Physiology

Information and Decision Sciences

Business Computing I
Business Systems Simulation
Business Statistics
Quality and Productivity Improvement Using Statistical Methods
Management Information Systems
Computer Performance Evaluation and Modeling
Operations Management
Operations Research

Italian

Conversational Italian
Italian Composition and Conversation
Introduction to Reading and Analysis of Italian Literary Texts
Advanced Italian Composition and Conversation
Advanced Italian Grammar
Modern Italian Literature and Society
Literary Forms in the Early Renaissance
Contemporary Italian Literature
Divine Comedy
Italian Phonetics

Italian Culture and Civilization
History of the Italian Language

Kinesiology

Biology of Cells and Organisms
Introduction to Psychology
English Composition I, II
Interpersonal Communication
Introduction to the Kinesiology Profession
Fundamental Movement Skills
Human Physiological Anatomy I, II
Philosophical and Psycho-Social Aspects of Movement
Functional Anatomy
Physiology of Exercise
Perceptual-Motor Learning and Development
Evaluation in Physical Education and Health

Latin American Studies

Introduction to Latin America in a World Context
Introduction to Contemporary Latin America
Expository Writing on Latin American Topics
Latin America since 1850
Mexico since 1850
History of Modern Puerto Rico
Central American Culture and Literary Studies
Topics in Latino Community Studies
Problems of South American Ethnology
Latinas in the United States

Management

Organizational Analysis and Practice
Organizational Behavior
Human Resource Management
Labor-Management Relations
Negotiation and Conflict Resolution
Compensation and Reward Systems
Career Planning and Development

Managerial Effectiveness through Diversity
Impact of Technological Change
Industrial Sociology

Marketing

Consumer Market Behavior
Marketing Research and Information Systems
Marketing Management
Principles of Retailing
Small Business Consulting
The Personal Selling Effort in Marketing
Advertising and Sales Promotion
Product Management
Comparative Marketing Systems

Mathematics

Calculus for Mathematics, Engineering, and Science I, II, III
Writing for Mathematics
Linear Algebra
Abstract Algebra
Advanced Calculus I, II
Complex Analysis with Applications
Formal Logic

Mechanical Engineering

Statistics
Strength of Materials
Fortran Programming for Engineers
Electrical Circuit Analysis
Engineering Economy
Engineering Graphics and Design
Thermodynamics
Dynamics of Rigid Bodies
Fluid Mechanics I, II
Technical Vibrations
Mechanisms and Dynamics of Machinery
Heat Transfer

Experimental Methods in ME
Manufacturing Process Principles
Senior Design
Introduction to Computer-Aided Design

Music

Music Theory I–IV
Ear Training I–IV
Keyboard Skills I–IV
Music History I, II, III
Counterpoint
Analytic Techniques
Jazz
Opera
Music for Symphony Orchestra
Composition
Conducting
Convocation/Recital
Concert Band
University Choir
Early Music Consort
Jazz Ensemble

Occupational Therapy

Human Physiological Anatomy I, II
Introduction to Psychology
Statistics in Psychology
Abnormal Psychology
Developmental Psychology
Classical Etymology in the Life Sciences
Occupational Therapy Fundamentals
Neurological Foundations of Occupational Performance I
Development of Occupational Performance I, II
Sociocultural Aspects of Occupational Therapy
Biomechanical Interventions I, II
Neurological Interventions with Children
Psychosocial Intervention I, II
Occupational Therapy Processes

Organizational Systems for Practice
Neurological Interventions with Adults
Research in Occupational Therapy

Philosophy

Introduction to Philosophy
Introductory Logic
Symbolic Logic
Ancient Philosophy I: Plato and His Predecessors
History of Modern Philosophy I: Descartes and His Successors
Medieval Philosophy
The Philosophy of Psychology
Metaphysics
Topics in Ethics and Political Philosophy
Morality and the Law
The Philosophy of Death
Understanding Art

Physical Therapy

Human Physiological Anatomy I
Introduction to Psychology
Statistics in Psychology
Neuroanatomy for Allied Health Professions
Gross Human Anatomy I, II
Physiology and Biophysics
Introduction to Physical Therapy
Communication, Education, and the Profession
Kinesiology
Therapeutic Exercise I, II
Physical Agents
Clinical Neurology
Orthopedics
Clinical Lectures in Psychiatry and Pediatrics
Clinical Instruction and Practice I, II, III
Community Resources for Health Care
Management
Critical Inquiry in Physical Therapy
Orthopedic Physical Therapy

Rehabilitation I, II
Culture and Rehabilitation
Pathophysiology

Physics

General Physics I–IV
Electromagnetism I
Quantum Mechanics I
Theoretical Mechanics I
Thermal and Statistical Physics
Mathematical Methods for Physicists
Modern Experimental Physics I

Polish

Polish Composition and Conversation I–IV
Introduction to Polish Literature I, II
Writing about Literature
Structure of Modern Polish
Studies in Polish Drama
Studies in Polish Literature
History of Poland
Mickiewicz and Sienkiewicz: Polish Romanticism and Realism

Political Science

Introduction to American Government and Politics
Introduction to Political Analysis I, II
American Political Theories
Introduction to International Relations
Topics in Comparative Politics
State Government
The Mass Media and Politics
Topics in Political Behavior
Possible Political Systems: Ideal and Actual

Psychology

Introduction to Psychology
Research in Psychology

Writing in Psychology
Statistical Methods in Behavioral Science
Cognition and Memory
Abnormal Psychology
Social Psychology
Theories of Personality
Learning
Developmental Psychology

Russian

Russian Composition and Conversation I–IV
Introduction to Russian Literature I, II
Writing about Literature
Structure of Modern Russian
Studies in the Russian Novel
Studies in Russian Literature
Dostoyevsky
Women in Russian Literature

Social Work

Introduction to Practice Skills
Practice I, II
Human Behavior and the Social Environment
Human Service Organizations in the Community
Majority and Minority Cultural Interaction
Social Welfare Policy and Services
Social Work Research
Field Instruction I, II
Integrative Seminar
Family Theory and Practice
Group Theory and Practice
Community Theory and Practice

Sociology

Introduction to Sociology
Introductory Sociological Statistics
Introduction to Sociological Research
Sociological Analysis

Explaining Social Life
Social Inequalities
Youth and Society
Gender and Society
African Americans and the Criminal Justice System
Industrial Society

Spanish

Conversational Spanish
Spanish Composition
Introduction to the Reading of Hispanic Texts
Introduction to the Analysis of Hispanic Texts
Advanced Spanish Composition
Advanced Spanish Grammar
Early Spanish Literature and Society
Modern Spanish Literature and Society
Spanish American Literature and Society
Writing and Research in the Major
History of the Spanish Language
Modern Spanish Literature I, II

Theater

Introduction to Theater
Theater Production
Fundamentals of Acting
Script Analysis
Design for the Stage
Drama in Its Cultural Context I, II
Stage Direction
Characterization
Advanced Acting: Classical Greek through Shakespeare
Practicum in Acting
Modern American Theater
Asian Theater Traditions
Scene and Lighting Design
The Actor's Voice
Costume and Makeup Design
Audition Technique
Stage Direction

NEW, UNUSUAL, AND DESIGN-YOUR- OWN MAJORS

Some majors weren't around in your parents' day: women's studies, urban planning, sports management. Majors have evolved because society evolves. The new majors may be a response to areas that have become marketable and are tied to the prospect of jobs. Others, such as the study of gender, result from philosophical evolution. Many are interdisciplinary, which means that you attend classes in several different departments and broaden your understanding of a field.

A description of some of the newer majors follows, as well as descriptions of ones you won't find on every campus. Then, of course, there is the option of designing your own major, an alternative offered at some schools. Perhaps you will find something here you did not know existed. At the very least, it should make you aware of a wide range of choices. Perhaps you will inquire about whether your area of interest is available in a new major at the school you are attending or planning to attend.

Toy Design

Just because you're going to college doesn't mean you have to give up your Legos, Etch-A-Sketch, or American Girl dolls. Bring them along as icons of design inspiration while at the Fashion Institute of Technology in New York City. Students may study a number of design majors including toys, advertising, fabric, fashion, illustration, interiors, packaging, apparel, and others. If you opt for toys, your curriculum will include Marker Rendering, Soft Toy and Doll Design, Motor Learning, Hard Toys, Computer Technology, Probability and Geometry, Toy Business Practices, and Toy Advertising and Promotion. Perhaps you will design the next Tickle Me Elmo.

Multilingual Journalism

Another interdisciplinary program, the Multilingual Journalism degree program at Lehman College, part of the City University of New York, brings together the departments of languages and literature, art, English, speech and theater, and black studies. Students enrolled in this program must take 12 credits of advanced foreign language courses, 9 credits of English, 9 credits of mass communication, and 12 credits of multilingual journalism. Students graduating with this degree are prepared to cover ethnic areas of the United States or to report on events in foreign countries.

Among the courses offered in this major are:

The Italian-American Community
Anthropological Linguistics
Inequality in Cross-Cultural Perspectives
Afro-Caribbean Heritage
Black Women in American Society
Migration & the Puerto Rican Community in the U.S.
The Economy of Puerto Rico
Television Directing
Broadcast Programming
American Jewish History
The Mainland Borough: The Bronx as a City in History

Human Ecology

College of the Atlantic in Bar Harbor, Maine, only has one major: human ecology. Don't apply if you want to pursue a major in any other subject.

In addition to the 36 credit hours in subjects pertaining to human ecology, students must complete a community service experience, spend at least one term in an internship related to their academic or professional goals, and write a human ecology essay, which describes the student's development as a human ecologist and demonstrates competence in writing.

In addition to a freshman year adviser, students are expected to form other relationships with faculty in order to develop significant courses of study. By senior year, students are expected to work closely with a two- or three-person team in preparation for graduation. Members of the team must include one teaching faculty member and one student, and, optionally, may include a third person from the faculty. Flexibility is honored. If one adviser doesn't fit, students are urged to seek out another and to consult faculty members frequently as questions arise and decisions must be made. The curriculum is organized into three resource areas: arts and design, environmental science, and human studies. Two courses from each of the resource areas are required, each by a different instructor.

Among the course listings are:

Conservation of Endangered Species
Functional Vertebrate Anatomy
Animal Behavior
Computer Assisted Data Analysis
Electronic Photography Studio
Politics and Communication: The Mexican Mass Media as an
    Ecosystem
The Eye and the Poet
Understanding Culture through Photography
Culture of Maine Woodworkers
Cultural Ecology of Population Control Practices
Contemporary Psychology: Development of Ecological Perspective
Modern Architecture: Survey of the 19th and 20th Centuries
The Aesthetics of Violence
History of Western Music

Nature, People and Property: An Introduction to Political Economy
Women/Men in Transition
Weed Ecology
Agroecology
Environmental Journalism

Leadership Studies

Abraham Lincoln had no formal training in leadership, but today colleges are offering a major in this area to help students learn leadership skills. Apparently, there is a dearth of leadership in the world with few people ready to step into the shoes of Winston Churchill, Mother Theresa, or Martin Luther King, Jr.

At the University of Richmond's Jepson School of Leadership Studies, the definition of leadership is "service not power or glory." Among the subjects that students take are group dynamics, motivation, conflict resolution, and communication and leading.

At Alverno College, a women's college in Milwaukee, the major is called Community Leadership and Development. The curriculum is designed to develop abilities to:

- Creatively address social problems with effective management skills
- Conduct financial analyses and social scientific research to reach solutions
- Explore the moral and ethical dimensions of community issues
- Draw on diverse political and cultural perspectives to develop your own philosophy
- Evaluate the effectiveness of different approaches to solving community needs

Courses for this program are offered in Alverno's Weekend College, every other weekend.

Therapeutic Riding

A positive interaction between physically and emotionally disabled people and horses is the focus of the therapeutic riding major. Through this relationship specialists in this field help promote the healing process. A **barrier-free campus** means providing ready access to both the buildings and to the information that is central to teaching and learning. One of the first barrier-free campuses, St. Andrews College in Laurinburg, North Carolina, has the first and only therapeutic riding major in the United States. A church-related institution, St. Andrews is committed to accommodating students with physical challenges.

The therapeutic riding major provides career training for the disabled, as well as the able-bodied student. Students learn how to manage and understand horses, develop their skills as riders; understand the theory of riding instruction; communicate orally and in written form; understand the safety, medical management, and ethical issues necessary in this field; and develop knowledge of the various disabling conditions and the practical applications of horseback riding as a therapeutic modality.

With a therapeutic riding business management degree, graduates can become a therapeutic riding facility manager, program manager or operator, or a therapeutic operations manager or development officer.

Peace Studies

As a response to issues in the escalating arms race and the war in Vietnam, Colgate University in Hamilton, New York, formed the peace studies program in 1970. According to the school's catalog, "The program promotes a rigorous academic approach to the issues of war and peace, conflict and social change, violence and nonviolence, using specialized research in the interdisciplinary field of peace studies in combination with relevant work in the social sciences and other disciplines. The overall aim of peace studies is to understand obstacles to peace, evaluate a range of solutions, and explore practical approaches to confronting the real conflicts of today."

With a degree in peace studies students may work in international agencies and nongovernmental organizations concerned with human rights and conflict resolution. As the catalog states, graduates may work in "international agencies and nongovernmental organizations concerned with peace and war, development, conflict resolution, and human rights. Work for such agencies is often integrated with professional careers in law, journalism, the media, education, and community organizing." Courses in this major include:

Movements for Peace and Social Change
Conflict Resolution and Mediation
Women and Peace: War, Resistance and Justice
Images of War and Peace in Twentieth-Century Art, Literature and Film
Peace and War: The European Experience

A peace studies major is also offered at Long Island University in its Friends World Program, Brooklyn Campus.

The program emphasizes that merely a desire to bring about positive change without the necessary education can actually worsen the situation in Third World countries. To empower its students, the program focuses on recognizing the source of conflict, developing strategies for its resolution, and recognizing the complexities of conflict resolution.

Students spend their first year in London, preparing for their second and third years, which are spent in other countries in what the program calls the "world university." The fourth year is spent back at Long Island University to reflect on the previous years' experiences with peers.

Here are some possibilities for the second and third years abroad, according to the New York Friends World Program Center's Web site:

> Students have studied and compared Gandhian nonviolence in India and Buddhist responses to oppression among Tibetan refugees. Others have compared feminist movements in Africa, Europe, and the United States. Game parks and natural resource management in Africa and India have been studied from the perspectives of local residents, nongovernmental organizations, and national economic and political aims.

Culture, Brain, and Development

Students who have an interest in human development might want to query Hampshire College in Amherst, Massachusetts, about its culture, brain, and development program. This program links multiple disciplines to study the process of development, including cognitive science, social sciences, and natural sciences.

This unique program is funded by a five-year grant from the Foundation for Psychocultural Research and boasts many cross-school courses. This offers students a chance to go beyond the nature-versus-nurture debate to view human development within a context of biology and culture, focusing on multiple perspectives from various fields, such as anthropology, psychology, biology, and neuroscience.

Courses include:

The Archaeology of Children
The Plastic Brain: Culture, Experience & Environment in Mind/Brain
    Development
Creating Families
African American Cognitive Science
Performance and Ethnography
Historical and Contemporary Perspectives on Reproduction and In-
    fant Development
Neuropathology
Archaeology of Disease
Culture, Mind, and Brain
Brain and Cognition II
Infant Development

Emergency Administration and Planning

Disasters, unfortunately, are a part of life. But now, people with a major in emergency administration and planning are ready and able to deal with these tragedies. The University of North Texas in Denton, Texas, claims to be the only university in the United States to offer such an undergraduate degree. According to one of the school's Web pages: "By majoring in emergency administration and planning, students become skilled in disaster planning, interpersonal communication and leadership. Students may opt to study emergency management at the local, state and federal government levels and nonprofit organization by choosing electives in public administration. Others may desire to focus on emergency preparedness in private organizations by selecting elective courses in business administration."

The faculty consists of individuals from a wide variety of education and professional backgrounds who have experience in varying sectors of emergency management.

As with so many of the newer majors, this one, too, is an interdisciplinary degree.

Synoptic Majors

If you have a substantial interest in a subject, such as world hunger, that crosses departmental boundaries, you may be able to design your own major at Kenyon College in Gambier, Ohio. The synoptic (think *synopsis*) major is for students whose interests lie between or among departments and allows them to combine a study of two or more subjects. The world hunger major combines biology, economics, and sociology. Other recent synoptic majors have combined course work in biology, chemistry, and psychology to form behavioral psychology; classics, history, and religion to form Middle East studies.

By the end of sophomore year, students wishing to pursue a synoptic major must think through how materials from selected courses would fit together, initiate a proposal, gather faculty advice, and submit their plan.

Turfgrass Management

Under the category of crop and soil sciences, students at Michigan State University in East Lansing, Michigan, may major in turfgrass management. In this major students study urban agriculture. The knowledge of the biological and physical sciences has expanded and improved the use of land. At the same time scientists have found ways to increase plant adaptation to environmental and other stresses. As a result, graduates of this program find jobs in industries involved in management of lawns, athletic fields, golf courses, parks, and ground maintenance. In pursuing this major students take the following courses: Plant Biology, Chemistry, Plant Genetics, Management of Turfgrass Pests, Soil Fertility, Principles of Weed Science, to name a few.

Aeronautical Science

The Wright brothers were the first to soar with the birds. Their flight in 1903 stirred imaginations and the desire for aeronautical education. The Embry-Riddle School of Aviation was formed in 1926 in Cincinnati. Three years later, the school became a subsidiary of AVCO, the parent of American Airlines. In the 1930s, the Great Depression kept the school dormant, only to become a needed source of education for pilots and mechanics during World War II.

Today, the locations at Daytona Beach, Florida, and at a second campus in Prescott, Arizona, offer many mild-weather days to gain flying experience. The school's promotional motto is, "There is one university—one—where everyone aims at the stars." Among the majors offered are aviation business administration, space physics, aerospace engineering, global security and intelligence studies, engineering physics, avionics engineering technology, aerospace studies, aeronautical science, and aviation maintenance management.

The field's most sophisticated flight training devices, which replicate Cessnas, Pipers, and Regional Jets, and 41 flight simulators enable the students to simulate flying experiences. Flight instruction is given in a fleet of 3 Cessna 150s, 62 Cessna 172s, 2 Cessna 182RGs, 6 Piper PA28R Arrows, 18 Piper PA44 Seminoles, and 2 American Champion Decathlons.

The school also offers degree programs to working adults in the evenings, weekends, and online at its Extended Campus with more than 120 teaching sites in the United States and Europe.

Bachelor of Arts in Engineering

Usually an engineering major has to sacrifice the benefits of a liberal arts education in order to complete all the required courses in his or her specialty. Not at Lafayette College in Easton, Pennsylvania, where the two disciplines have been combined in an innovative program. Called the AB in Engineering, the degree does not prepare students to practice as engineers but rather for careers in law, architecture, public policy, medicine, technical sales, technical writing, project construction, information systems, and environmental management in which a technical background is a recognized asset.

The difference between an AB degree and a BS degree is broken down at the college as:

	AB	BS
Mathematics and physical science	8 courses	8 courses
Technical	11 courses	22 courses
Humanities and social science	13 courses	8 courses

According to the catalog, the Bachelor of Arts in engineering degree blends a background of math and science with an understanding of human behavior and a sensitivity to the human condition through courses in history, literature, language and philosophy, psychology, sociology, and political science.

Residential Property Management

In response to industry demand for more and better-trained professionals in the housing industry, a residential property management major was established in 1985 by Virginia Tech, in Blacksburg, Virginia. So strong was the industry's commitment that more than $200,000 has been donated by industry professionals to support the program.

In addition to courses in the humanities, the degree requires 45 credits in property management, including the following courses: Family Housing, Maintenance for Property Managers, Barrier-Free Design, Survey of Accounting, Contemporary Issues in Property Management, and Marketing Management. Students may take the following courses as electives: Real Estate Law, Issues in Aging, Organization Behavior, and Public Speaking. Local property management firms provide paid internships to access extra help during busy times of the year and to review a potential pool of future employees. Graduates manage income-producing properties such as apartment communities, shopping centers, and office buildings. Because Virginia Tech has one of the only RPM programs in the country, students are in great demand when they graduate, according to Dr. Rosemary Goss, Professor of Housing.

Hawaiian Studies

You can actually major in Hawaii! Since many people believe that it doesn't matter what you major in, as long as you develop skills critical to life success, why not study an island in the Pacific? This major, offered at the University of Hawai'i at Manoa, offers the following courses: Hawaiian Genealogies, Chiefs of Post-Contact Hawai'i, Myths of Hawaiian History, and Pana O'ahu: Famous Place Names. The last is a survey of the famous place names in each 'ahupua'a of O'ahu, including accounts of mythical heroes, heiau, fish ponds, wind, rain names and their metaphoric value in Hawaiian literature.

Sport Sciences

Most sports are big business today, and getting into any of these popular fields requires preparation. At Ohio State University in Athens, Ohio, home of the Buckeyes, the sports sciences major requires students to study business and economics, sports management, courses relating to First Aid, behavioral sciences, and sports industry electives. Electives include:

American Baseball to 1930
American Baseball since 1930
Labor Relations
The Black Athlete and American Sports
Administration of Aquatic Facilities

Graduates with a major in sport sciences lead programs at every educational level, manage recreational facilities and clubs, and they coach serious athletes.

Bagpiping

One of the reasons Carnegie Mellon University in Pittsburgh gives for its major in bagpiping is that no opportunities existed anywhere in the world for the serious student of bagpipes to get conservatory training. Students of voice, jazz, keyboard, and band instruments have ample opportunities at many campuses.

Then, there was the fact that Andrew Carnegie, the founder of the university, had a rich Scottish tradition and was also, well, rich. Coincidentally, a famous bagpiper, James McIntosh, had moved his bagpiping business from Maryland to be director of the pipe band. He had taught extensively in Australia, France, Scotland, Canada, and the United States and is a well-known authority on the classical music of the bagpipe, *piobaireachd*. So, Carnegie Mellon became the first conservatory in the world to offer a complete classical program of music study leading to a Bachelor of Fine Arts degree in music performance with bagpipes as the principal instrument. Students have private studio instruction in bagpipes and professional training in bagpipe reed making. They also learn maintenance and the history of the instrument.

They must participate in the choral program and study complete instruction in music theory, solfege (applying the sof-fa syllables to a musical scale or melody), eurhythmics, music history, piano and performing ensembles and a wide range of courses available as general studies electives. You can catch performances by the Carnegie Mellon Pipe and Drum Band at football games, commencement, and other campus events. Many in the pipe band had never played the pipes before coming to Carnegie Mellon.

Electronic Media, Arts, and Communication

Describing itself as "the first program of its kind anywhere in the country," Rensselaer Polytechnic Institute in Troy, New York, is offering a state-of-the-art electronic media, arts, and communication major. A hybrid of electronic communication and electronic art, it trains students for jobs in a cross-section of "virtual" industries, including computer graphics, hyper media, cyberspace and virtual reality, Web design and authoring, the electronic arts and multimedia, and animation and game design.

This new type of interdisciplinary program aims to produce entrepreneurs who will use technology in innovative ways in industry and the arts. At Rensselaer, the goal is to train students for leadership in a rapidly transforming information society.

Visual Effects and Motion Graphics

Offered at the Art Institute of Phoenix, these interrelated fields deal with design, layering, and movement of the digital imagery needed to tell a visual story. Motion graphics is graphic design for broadcast and film, while visual effects uses computer software to bring various images into a single believable scene. The Art Institute of Phoenix, one of a for-profit group of 31 colleges called the Art Institutes, offers advertising, culinary arts, fashion marketing, interior design, and other visual communication majors. Students do not need to take national exams such as the SAT or ACT for admission.

International Theater Production

Ohio Northern University in Ada, Ohio, offers students interested in studying theater production a unique degree—Bachelor of Fine Arts in communication arts with a concentration in international theater production. In addition to studying theatrical design, production, and stage management, students are also required to study a foreign language and topics in international studies. They must also complete an international internship or study abroad for a semester.

The program also hires ten nationally and internationally acclaimed guest directors, choreographers, and designers per year. Guests in the past include artists from Scotland, Iceland, Estonia, Portugal, Ireland, and England. Ohio Northern University believes that this international element facilitates students' exposure to diverse global methodologies and development of a broad understanding of the theater arts, including touring, production, and opera.

Another benefit that the program offers to students, according to the university, is the opportunity to be involved with hosting an international festival: "Every year we host an International Playwrighting Festival. We commission 15 to 20 minute works from different international playwrights which we produce in an evening of One Acts. In 2004, the playwrights were from Chile, Cuba and Mexico with a Mexican director. In 2005 we will feature works from the Pacific Rim."

Interactive Media and Game Development

At the Worcester Polytechnic Institute in Cambridge, Maine, students may pursue their love of computer games by majoring in interactive media and game development. This brand new program was developed by WPI during 2004 and offered for the first time in 2005 through examination of the International Game Developers Association Curriculum Framework, other educational programs, and through dialogue with members of the game development industry.

This program is different from many other majors in that it is interdisciplinary and draws from two very distinct fields—arts and humanities (art, music, and story) and computer science (technical, programming). After studying a core of the art and technical aspects of interactive media and game development, students may select either an artistic or a technical concentration.

Advanced courses in concentration areas include:

Art and Animation
Artistic Game Development I and II
Critical Studies of Interactive Media and Games
Digital Imaging and Computer Art
Essentials of Art
The Game Development Process
Philosophy and Ethics of Computer Games
Social Issues in Interactive Media and Games
Storytelling in Interactive Media and Games
Technical Game Development I and II

Students will also study the social and philosophical issues surrounding the industry. In addition to a rigorous curriculum, by requiring students concentrating in art and science to work closely with one another, this program prepares students for the reality of work in this field. By the end of the program, students will have completed two large projects—one software project and one group project in which students concentrate on both technical and artistic areas. Students in this major will be well prepared for a career in the interactive media, art, or computer programming industries.

Intercultural Studies for Business

Created by Wofford College in Spartanburg, South Carolina, the intercultural studies for business program combines an education in business with a liberal arts education to prepare students for today's international business community.

In this program, students study the business basics—math, economics, accounting, and finance—as well as a foreign language and culture. Students may choose German, French, or Spanish for their foreign language. The foreign language study is extensive. In addition to taking basic and advanced foreign language and culture classes, students also are required to spend at least one semester abroad. Furthermore, they spend one semester studying international businesses and visiting local international businesses; Spartanburg County boasts many international businesses, including BMW's North American manufacturing facility.

Health Communications

Grand Valley State in Allendale, Michigan, offers one of the nation's only undergraduate health communication programs. According to the school, "The health communicator has the vital role of facilitating communications between aware but technically naive consumers and a system that is operated by highly skilled, deeply educated technical professionals whom the public does not fully understand."

Students interested in studying communications may specialize their knowledge through study of health sciences as well as courses in advertising, public relations, journalistic and public relations writing, and visual media to work in the changing health industry.

With a degree in health communication, graduates may find jobs in hospitals, pharmaceutical companies, HMOs, and state and local health departments among other health-related organizations and corporations.

Courses offered include:

Public Health Concepts
Medical Terminology
Health Care Management
News Reporting I
Health Communication Systems

Adventure Recreation

Green Mountain College in Poultney, Vermont, offers an exciting major that prepares students for careers in the growing adventure recreation industry, through developing leadership skills and preparing them for management-level positions. In addition, students may opt to complete various national organizations' certification courses.

Certifications students may choose from are: whitewater canoe, kayak, or rafting instructors (American Canoe Association)

Adventure program facilitators (Project Adventure)
Open water dive instructors (Professional Association of Dive Instructors)
Mountain guides (American Mountain Guide Association)
Skiing/snowboarding instructors (Professional Ski Instructors of America)

Lesbian, Gay, and Bisexual Studies

Hobart and William Smith in Geneva, New York offers one of the nation's first majors in lesbian, gay, and bisexual studies. This interdisciplinary course of study integrates cross-divisional perspectives in addition to pointing out the universality of issues related to lesbian, gay, and bisexual individuals, such as identity and control over the self. The program offers classes dealing specifically with lesbian, gay, and bisexual issues and offers the following courses: Sexual Minorities in America and Gender in Antiquity. The program also deals with broader topics and offers Readings in Multi-Ethnic Women's Literature and Self in American Culture as courses. The program requires that students complete an internship, independent study, or honors project that integrates material from all their studies.

In addition to those mentioned above, course offerings include:

Literature of Sexual Minorities
Sexual Minority Movements and Public Policy
Que (e) rying Religious Studies
Ghettoscapes
Feminist Legal Theory
Spanish Cinema: Buñuel to Almodóvar
Beyond Monogamy
Life-Cycles: The Family in History
Sexuality and American Literature

Equestrian Business Management

Horse-loving students can earn a degree in equestrian business management at Stephens College in Columbia, Missouri. This program combines a strong liberal arts education with 18 hours of business courses, 34 hours of equestrian courses, and Red Cross certification to thoroughly prepare graduates for careers in the horse industry.

Courses include:

Riding: 5 classes
Equine Management
Methods of Teaching Horsemanship I, II, and III
Show Horse Preparation
Horse Keeper
Equine Feeding and Nutrition
Stable Management
Theory of Horseshoeing
Equestrian Business Management

Graduates of this program may become managers, teachers, or trainers in the horse industry.

Ranch Management

Established in 1956 with input from southwestern ranchers, the ranch management program offered by Texas Christian University in Fort Worth, Texas, prepares students to manage ranches with both in classroom instruction and extensive field study. According to the program's mission statement, the program aims, "To prepare students as lifelong learners to manage a wide range of resources anywhere in the world on an ecologically and economically sound basis for continuing maximum net return while conserving and improving the resources."

This rigorous program prepares students to manage agricultural resources in a rapidly changing industry and includes field trips throughout Texas, Oklahoma, and Kansas.

Courses include:

Ranch Operations & Development
Soil & Water Conservation

Beef Cattle Production
Animal Health Management
Range Management
Ranch Records & Finance
Animal Nutrition & Feeding
Sheep & Goat Production
Animal Health & Reproduction
Marketing Livestock & Meats
Forage Production & Use

Fisheries

Mansfield University in Mansfield, Pennsylvania, offers a degree in fisheries, a preparation for careers dealing with salmon, cod, and catfish, among other types of fish. Raising fish in a fishery is a complex science and requires a science-based education. A program within the biology department, courses required for this program include Ecology, Ichthyology, Cell Biology, Microbiology, Zoology, General Chemistry, and Physics, among others. In addition, students are required to complete an internship, field courses, and a research project. Graduates are ready to be certified as Associate Fisheries Scientists by the American Fisheries Society and may also receive American Fisheries Society Certification by taking a statistics course offered by Mansfield University.

Design Your Own Major

These new and unusual majors illustrate that a wide array of choices awaits students of every interest. Investigate on your own. Whether it's gerontology, the specialty of working with the aged, or musicology that interests you, colleges are dynamic places that incorporate change to serve the needs of students and society.

Sarah Lawrence College

There are no declared majors at Sarah Lawrence College, a liberal arts college for women and men in Bronxville, New York. Instead, with the help of an adviser (called a *don*), students design their own curricula.

Each student's program consists of three courses, most of which are seminars, of no more than 15 students, allowing for intensive study in each field. Students attend individual student-faculty meetings every week in their first-year studies course. For each seminar, students complete a conference project—an independent study that results in a substantial research paper or project—in addition to their class work. Students typically spend at least 15 hours a week studying for each course, for which they earn 10 semester hours of credit a year. Most courses are full-year courses.

Students rarely ask to see grades in the registrar's office unless they are applying for graduate school. Instead, growth and achievement of the student are evaluated in reports written by faculty and sent to the students and their advisers twice a year. In these statements, faculty members report their judgment of the student's academic achievement, attitude toward work, study habits, ability to learn and form judgments and to use what is learned, ability to work independently—all the factors that show a student's intellectual progress.

Meira Kensky became interested in Sarah Lawrence when she heard about it on television. In her second semester there she wrote a 30-page paper on the freedom of religion clauses in the First Amendment to the Constitution, which involved designing the project, and reading 40 to 50 Supreme Court opinions plus other articles.

"Everyone is writing papers all the time but feels free to take a studio art class or read Nabakov. If you want to know your grade point average, you can calculate it yourself or ask for it, but people aren't constantly freaking about grade point," she said.

Evergreen State College

Coordinated studies, in which students and faculty from different disciplines join to answer a question or solve a problem, are the beginning of academic life at the Evergreen State College in Olympia, Washington. Freshmen gain a solid foundation of knowledge and skills in these programs, designed especially to prepare them for advanced studies in a wide range of subject areas. Plus, freshmen have the opportunity to work with a wide mix of students—in age, experience, and stages of learning. Core programs introduce students to Evergreen's interdisciplinary studies approach; they learn how to write more effectively, read more carefully, analyze arguments, reason both quantitatively and mathematically, work cooperatively in small groups, and use campus resources such as the library. In addition, freshmen can explore all-level programs, which enroll a mix of freshmen through seniors, and some programs for sophomores and above may admit a particularly well-qualified freshman.

Among courses offered to freshmen are:

American Frontiers
Critical Histories
Asian Culture and Art: Buddhist Psychotherapy
Consuming Utopia: From Wilderness to Wal-Mart
Growing Up Global
History and Evolution of Disease
Madness and Creativity, the Psychological Link

The core program also allows students to link studies with their own intellectual and personal concerns.

Following is a description of the course, "The Physicist's World," which is an all-level program offering appropriate support for freshmen as well as supporting and encouraging those ready for advanced work.

The 20th century has brought about a revolution in our understanding of the physical universe. We have been forced to revise the way we think about even such basic concepts as space and time and causality, and about the properties of matter. An important part of this revolution has been the surprising discovery of fundamental ways in which our knowledge of the material world is ultimately limited. These limitations are not the result of surmountable shortcomings in human understanding, but are more deeply rooted in the nature of the universe itself. In this program, we will examine the mental world created by the physicist so that we can make sense out of our experience of the material world, and try to understand the nature of physical reality. We will ask and explore answers to the twin questions of epistemology: What can we know? How can we know it? Starting with the Presocratic philosophers, we will continue through each major development of 20th-century physics, including the theories of relativity, quantum theory, deterministic chaos and modern cosmology. We will examine the nature and the origins of the limits that each theory imposes on our ultimate knowledge of the world. We will read primary texts, such as works by the Presocratics, Plato, Lucretius, Galileo, Newton and Einstein, as well as selected contemporary Writings on physics. In addition to the other texts, a book-length manuscript has been written for this program that will serve as an extended outline and guide to the works and ideas we will read and discuss. Fall quarter will concentrate on the period up to the beginning of the 20th century; winter quarter will cover developments during the 20th century.

No mathematical prerequisites are assumed. Mathematical thinking will be developed within the context of the other ideas as needed for our purposes. The only prerequisites are curiosity about the natural world and a willingness to read and think and write about challenging texts and ideas. The program is preparatory for careers and futures in the humanities and sciences.

Marlboro College

A small and innovative liberal arts college in Vermont, Marlboro offers each student a highly individualized program of study. Students design their own majors, and most of them are multidisciplinary. Recent students have combined biology and theater, international studies and dance, creative writing and sociology.

One of the newer colleges in the United States, Marlboro College was founded in 1947 by a handful of veterans who transformed two Vermont Hill farms into classrooms, dorms, and a dining hall. The original student body of 50 has grown to include 336 students who come to Vermont for individualized education.

The academic program is based on the "plan of concentration," a program in which students explore a field of interest and conclude with a major independent project that aims to solve a problem or answer a question of vital interest to the student. Students work with faculty in one-on-one individualized tutorials designed to instruct them in an area not normally covered in the regular course schedule. Before graduation students must defend their plans in a two- or three-hour oral exam before Marlboro faculty members and an outside examiner from another institution who is expert in the subject area of the plan.

"I remember saying at a certain point that I wanted to be on Plan for the rest of my life. I always want to be searching for conclusions, finding out about things. I had never worked hard in my life until I was working on my Plan, and I had never really grown in terms of my ability to reason until Marlboro," said Sean Cole who was graduated from Marlboro with a creative writing and theater plan of concentration.

Stop, Look, and Consider Your Many Choices

If you don't think you will fit into a traditional curriculum and no major "feels right," a design- your-own major may be your best choice. Ask at each school you apply to whether such an option is available.

CHOOSE A MAJOR, THEN CONCENTRATE ON SKILLS

Choosing a major is merely choosing a label. As the job market has changed and many people are in jobs that have nothing to do with their major, career counselors at the colleges are advising students to concentrate on skill development. "I've had students in liberal arts graduate without picking up one skill," complained one career counselor.

You'll be able to acquire some of the skills you need by merely rubbing shoulders on campus with professors and other students. Others will require a concerted effort on your part to develop before graduation.

Building skills will enrich your life and make you marketable to different employers. In the old days students learned skills at college, but the transferability of these skills to different jobs wasn't recognized. Today, when considering a new position, employees carry a bag of skills from job to job

Review the following skills that employers say they want in their employees. Determine which ones you already have and which ones you need to develop.

Presentation Skills

"I get too nervous to speak in front of a group of people."

Only 1 person in 25 is comfortable with public speaking, but presentation skills will put you way ahead of the pack in your career. At first, getting up in front of any group seems more painful than setting yourself on fire. David Letterman said in an interview that his ego rises and falls on each night's performance. However, your good ideas will be lost if you can't present them in front of other people.

Besides speaking in front of a group, students need interpersonal presentation skills. You need to be able to get your ideas across in class, in conferences with instructors, in small groups. If you can't verbalize your thoughts to others, they lose the benefit of your ideas. Some students would rather have their hair pulled out than say a word in class.

Zack was a stutterer in high school, but he now readily volunteers his ideas in classroom discussions. He achieved this, he says, by forcing himself to make speeches and speak up whenever he saw an opportunity. He made up his mind to attack this problem and now presents better than most college seniors.

Understanding the nuances of words and expressions, body language, the appropriateness of behaviors, these are skills that students learn more fully in college, mainly by interacting with many different people. To develop excellent presentation skills, you must:

1. Develop something interesting to say: original, thought-provoking, entertaining
2. Understand the needs of your audience, whether it's one person or many people
3. Practice whenever you get a chance

> Seize every opportunity to speak in front of others. Each time you do you will be putting money in your career bank.

Listening Skills

Pay attention. Much learning occurs through listening. In large lecture halls, in study groups, in one-on-one conversations, the ability to listen intently to the information being presented is important for success in college and later in your career. When someone else is talking, many people are thinking about what they are going to say next instead of really capturing what the speaker is saying. A good way to enhance your listening skills is to devote one day to really listening to whatever people are saying. Not only will you improve your listening skills, but you'll score points with the speakers. People appreciate being heard and being paid attention to.

> Spend one day listening to people, not talking.

Communication Skills

A cat communicates through purring, crouching, or hissing. As human beings, we have broader and more specific communication techniques at our disposal: body language, voice, gesture, words, appearance. A cat can't explain nuances of its purr. Many of our communications—slouching, crossing arms across the chest, whistling, or shifting eye contact—undermine our attempts to connect with other people.

Your posture is an important communication tool. Did you ever notice the attentive posture of dogs? They never slouch because their survival depends on good listening skills. They are on alert. If they aren't, they might miss a potential meal. In the classroom the instructor immediately senses who is paying attention and who is not by the posture of students.

Thumbs up, thumbs down signal approval or disapproval. When someone gives you a hand gesture in traffic, you know that he or she disapproves of your driving. Resting your head on your arm in class means you are tired. Being aware of how our gestures communicate ideas to others is an important part of our skill repertoire.

> In front of a mirror, try to parody the gestures of others to see what they communicate.

Writing Skills

Writing works like a muscle in your body that needs constant exercise. Good writers work at building their writing muscle. Writing is one of the most tangible ways that we express ourselves, and expression takes time and effort. Become a regular at the writing center on campus. It's there for everyone, not just students who need remedial help. If you're taking a writing course, visit the instructor during office hours. Ask what you can do to improve your writing.

Many students are discouraged about their writing and fail to realize that published authors go through many drafts, revisions, and soul-searching to put the right words on paper. If you don't master this skill, it will haunt you throughout your career. The good news is that the more you write, the better you become. Unfortunately, the people who most need to develop this skill are afraid to write and be critiqued. Practice makes perfect, or at least better. When queried about which tasks they hate at work, employees put "writing" as one of the top tasks. This skill is doable for those who have the motivation to get started and realize that writing is a process that continues throughout life. You will be better than you are today.

You need the nourishment of reading in order to produce good writing. Even a half an hour a day devoted to reading for your own growth as a writer is well worth the effort. If you need inspiration, read *Bird by Bird, Some Instructions on Writing and Life* by Anne Lamott, Anchor Book Edition, 1995.

One aspect of writing that gives some people fits is spelling. The ability to spell words correctly has nothing to do with intelligence. With the use of spell-checkers in computer programs, much of the anxiety has been eliminated. However, keep in mind that the software won't tell you if you've selected the wrong word—it can't distinguish between "their" and "there," for example.

Another way to deal with spelling problems is to have someone help you—a good reader who will read your work and catch spelling and grammatical errors. Another pair of eyes is helpful for content also.

Phone Skills

In an effort to save time and money, many companies today conduct the first interview with a prospective employee over the phone. Frequently people are eliminated at this early point in the process because they have not developed good phone skills.

In addition to listening, the most important phone skill is enthusiasm. Many opportunities for you will be lost if you do not sound enthusiastic. A lukewarm reception to a potential employer's call makes the caller feel you are not interested. The recent graduate is probably not really lukewarm, but astonished that he or she has received a call after sending in a résumé. Or the person is nervous. Practice answering the phone with a positive voice and try to sound receptive to the person who is about to interview you. Even if you are not interested, it will be good practice.

Another problem on the phone is clarity. People leave messages with prospective employers and zoom over the return phone number. They are in a hurry to get off the phone and leave the receiver of the message wondering, "Who was that person?" "What did he want?" Polished professionals repeat the number they are leaving twice. This can save everyone a great deal of time and is part of phone skills.

Your tone of voice on the phone influences the listener. Ask friends to give you their impression of how you sound on the phone. One job applicant was rejected on the basis of his haughty-sounding tone on his answering machine. Sound friendly and positive.

Background noise can give the wrong impression. When you answer the phone, be sure to turn off music or the television. The sound of Radiohead blasting in the background may be distracting to the caller. A dog barking in the background also presents problems. Usually, the dog owner interrupts the conversation repeatedly to tell the dog to be quiet. Obviously, this does not project a professional, in-charge image. You can't even manage a dog, the caller thinks, perhaps only subconsciously.

Another part of phone skills is always to have paper and pen by the phone. Callers are usually on a schedule do not appreciate having to wait while you run upstairs to get writing supplies.

E-Mail Skills

People who normally write excellent letters with perfect spelling take all sorts of liberties with e-mail, thus leaving a bad impression. Just because e-mail is fast and convenient does not mean that it should be written without care. Be sure to read your e-mail messages carefully before you send them. Skill in e-mailing is part of being a complete professional.

Everyone has had the experience of pressing the wrong computer key, for instance, "Reply to all." Although the stories about how a highly personal memo was sent electronically to a group of people are funny, you don't want to be the source of the humor. So exercise care in all aspects of your e-mail activities.

Critical-Thinking Skills

Can you use information, reason, and experience to move from assumptions to applications to consequences? Bundled together, these critical-thinking skills equip employees to add value to their companies. Building critical-thinking skills means shedding preconceived notions. Shedding these notions opens the opportunity to look at a subject with a fresh perspective.

An important part of building critical-thinking skills is gathering information and knowing which sources are valid. In college students read the writings of many authors and hear lectures offering different viewpoints. In the dorms and in classrooms you will hear opinions much different from your own. In writing research papers, you must decide which position to take, find supporting arguments, and provide documentation. Critical thinking continues for the rest of your life. Developing this skill in college is a major task.

Interpersonal Skills

No matter how brilliant people are, they will be lost without interpersonal skills, the ability to get along with other people. In his best-selling book, *Emotional Intelligence: Why It Can Matter More Than IQ,*

Daniel Goleman, Bantam Books, 1997, says that achievers reach success by building a rapport with a network of key people who can be relied on when expert help is needed. In a crunch these people have contacts. He writes:

> But after detailed interviews, the critical differences emerged in the internal and interpersonal strategies 'stars' used to get their work done. One of the most important turned out to be a rapport with a network of key people. . . . They put time into cultivating good relationships with people whose services might be needed in a crunch as part of an instant ad hoc team to solve a problem or handle a crisis.

Shedding the shyness and self-consciousness of adolescence is part of the college experience. Ways to do this? Start talking to other people in class and begin to form study groups. Working together with other people on projects will build your confidence and team abilities. Studying together makes understanding the material infinitely easier. Human beings need one another. College is a natural place to work on your interpersonal skills.

Interpersonal skills, then, are a major learning task in college. Colleges are aware of the importance of these skills. Coincidentally, these skills serve the colleges' purpose of retention, keeping students enrolled. One of the prime reasons students stay at the college they selected is a sense of belonging. If they feel comfortable and can afford the tuition, they will stay. Whether this sense of belonging comes from joining the rock-climbing club or a sorority or from having great freshman roommates, students decide to return, saving the college a great deal of effort and recruitment funds.

You can test your own interpersonal skills by asking yourself the following questions:

- Have you met any interesting new people in the past three months?
- If so, have you made an effort to get to know them better?
- Do you write letters or send e-mail to people on a regular basis?
- Do you count on other people for new ideas?
- Can you think of ways to make your life more interesting? Do these include people?

Organizational Skills

How would you label yourself today? Very organized? Disorganized? The American culture values organized people and gives them higher salaries. Rewards go to individuals who come early to meetings, hand projects in on time, have backup plans in case the first one runs off into a ditch. These organized people seem to be in the minority, so they are valued as a rare commodity. Why? If you asked 10 people to give a pint of blood to your friend, wouldn't you value the ones who showed up on time, gave blood, and saved your friend's life? Having organizational skills means being the one people can count on to get things done. You anticipate the problems, you have a goal, you meet the deadline.

How do you become organized? Not overnight. Like other new skills, it takes time. One way to become organized is to evaluate your reaction mode. In plain English, do you react and act on everything? If you do, you are not organized. A million demands hit us every day. Learning to postpone acting on most of them is the beginning of developing organizational skill. Organization simply means knowing what is important to you and sticking to it.

Begin with a simple test. Are you always on time? always late? always early? Why? If you can answer that question, you are on your way to discovering your organizational strengths and weaknesses.

Let's say you want to get good grades this semester but you are also a social being with lots of temptations to party. You have to make up your mind: grades or fun? Usually, the truth is somewhere in the middle. Disorganized people, however, are in an all-or-nothing mode. They become disorganized when they completely throw out one goal for a new pursuit. Sticking with goals is not easy. When temptations come along, the organized person accepts them partly without completely abandoning already established goals.

Happily, organizational skills improve the longer you are in college. They must, or you would flunk out. You learn how to boomerang back to your main task after several interruptions. You learn how to prioritize in order to tackle the most important tasks first. Some college graduates feel that the diploma means learning to jump through many hoops.

Tools for Organization

Knowing your own body rhythm is a part of getting organized. If there are times of the day or month when you are not at your peak, you know not to overload responsibilities at those times.

See below for some suggestions for ways for help you get organized.

Notebooks and Calendars

Not too very long ago people could keep important dates and notes of things to do in their heads. Rarely is this the case today. Our world is just too busy for us to remember everything. Even 18-year-olds have to write dates down and make notes about other important things.

Most very organized people write the next day's plan the night before. Making a stress-avoidance plan at the first of the month helps ease some of the frustrations, parking tickets, and missed appointments so common in a fast-paced society.

Keep a calendar on which you can write appointments, note when things are due, and remind yourself of something that's coming up that you need to prepare for.

Realism about Time

Unrealistic ideas about how much time it takes to do things will make you constantly behind. Misjudged travel time, weather conditions, study requirements—everything takes more time than most people think. What you think will take two hours takes four. Time is a precious commodity that is sorely underestimated and undervalued. So try to be realistic in your estimates of time. Add extra time you think you won't need, just to be safe.

The Twin Time Thieves of Television and Netsurfing

Hours of meaningless activity can be spent in front of a television or surfing the Net. Rare is the person who spends less than five hours a day in front of one of those screens. They may be useful, entertaining, enlightening, even educational, but they do distract the person who's inclined to be disorganized.

Research Skills

You won't be able to graduate from college without having developed research skills. Merely figuring out what classes to take demands research. During the first semester freshman year, students learn to gather material from sources other than the classroom and write about it. Today, researching means having computer research skills as well as being able to gather information on a subject from other people. But beware of blindly using search engine research for your reports. Make sure that your sources are reliable and up-to-date.

Reading a newspaper regularly will help to increase your research skills. Americans are notorious for not knowing geography and being unaware of foreign events. Particularly with globalization, knowing about the world and the activities of people outside our own sphere of influence increases our ability to conduct research. A broad range of knowledge will help you determine what is important to investigate and what can be cast aside.

The world is too complex and sophisticated for you to know about everything. The newspaper is similar to a flashlight, illuminating things we should pay attention to, even for a few seconds. The mind keeps this information and brings it up when you need it to build information in research.

Libraries and information sources are changing so rapidly that it's important to keep up on the latest ways to gather research. Instead of being overwhelmed by how much is out there, remember that you need to know only what is relevant for your field. You don't need to know everything.

A Professional Vocabulary

Your major will provide you with a professional vocabulary. Every computer tech in the United States uses the same terminology, which is a foreign language to everyone else. Every major has its own language. Biologists use words such as *photomorphogenesis convergence, macromolecules,* and *clonal segments.* Chemists talk about *reactivity* and *kinetics.* English majors use *rhetoric, discourse,* and *genre.* Whichever major you choose, you will gain the skill of using a professional vocabulary. On job interviews, interviewers will expect you to be familiar with the vocabulary of your specialty. No problem.

Concentration

Older people say that the younger generation has a shorter attention span than previous generations. They blame it on MTV. They remember when reading and radio were the principal forms of entertainment and when television did not consume many hours of the day. When the work was done, they talked to their neighbors on the porch, played cards, shot pool at the corner saloon, made pies, did homework. Homework assignments were simpler and easier to do because there weren't as many distractions. The old folks didn't have DVDs, microwave ovens, cell phones, answering machines, or even credit cards. If they are correct, the ability to concentrate on what you want to learn is more difficult to achieve now than in the past.

In college you will develop the skill of concentration, the ability you need to gain new knowledge. Does retention require you to review the material once? Three times? Sixteen times? How much time does it take you to acquire new knowledge? What is the optimal setting for you to acquire this knowledge? Do you need low background music to keep you focused? Or do you need complete quiet? Do you need to study in the library to stay away from your friends? Find out the answers to these questions and then do whatever it takes to help you concentrate.

Coachability

Coachability, the ability to be coached, has become popular in education and job environments. If you can be coached into performing better, you possess coachability. Some people refuse to listen to those higher than them in authority. No matter what the directions are, they decide to do it their own way. Organizations run best with people who are willing to be coached.

A first good place to learn and build coachability skills is in college, although some people learn the skill in high school. The skill is not only doing what you have been asked to do, but also figuring out what the coach wants done without being told. The second is much more difficult. The people who get A's in the classroom often have an innate sense of what is important to study, what the professor cares about, and what is irrelevant in the professor's mind. These people are also good test takers because they know what is important to study without having to review everything.

People who have good coachability skills follow directions easily and do not complain about workload. They seem to be motivated to get the job done with a minimum of confusion. They are pleasant to be around because they are positive and goal-oriented. They also are flexible. In a fast-changing world, people have to adjust frequently to change. The coach (professor, boss) gives one set of directions one week, and, because of circumstances, changes them the next week. The coachable person knows that game plans change.

People with coachability skills do well in college because they accept the format of college and comply with the rules. This includes:

- Attending class regularly.
- Buying the textbooks required.
- Handing in assignments on time.
- Keeping track of what is due and when.
- Talking with the instructor when assignments or classes are not clear.
- Seeing advisers about graduating on time.
- Thinking of ways to fit in rather than causing academic problems for themselves.
- Learning what the rules are and following them.
- Quickly becoming familiar with the terrain and adapting.
- Being a member of a team and not trying to usurp the coach's authority.

Creativity

College takes people out of what they have known and places them into an exploration of the unknown. Individual families, communities, high schools, all support a common culture. Once you leave that arena and go off to college, even if it is a few blocks away, the expectations and possibilities change.

The knowledge not only of what is, but also of what can be, is essential in a college education. The skill of creating something new, whether it's in a test tube or on the printed page in a poem or in a marketing program for a widget, is a by-product of higher education. Walking across campus gives students the time to be away from the "real" world and in this escape provides time for original thoughts, new ways of doing old things, or thinking of new things to advance civilization.

"What if . . ." becomes the mantra of creativity after you graduate from school to offices, homes, Web pages, and boardrooms. To leave college without creativity means that you didn't learn an important skill when you were there.

Technological Skills

Almost every freshman orientation program includes exposure to the computer facilities on campus. Many of these facilities are underutilized by students who are computer phobic. It takes tremendous discipline to spend time each week in the computer facility learning new programs. Some students give up too easily. Computer mastery takes many hours and can be discouraging unless you are willing to accept the fact that learning this new technology takes time.

First, besides word processing, you need to know where to find information available on the Internet and how to evaluate and document it. The main task is to overcome computer phobia and realize that the learning curve on any program is very short—in two weeks you could learn all you need to know about any particular program.

Second, realize that you don't need to know everything that's out there. You only need to know the programs essential for getting your job of getting through school done.

Planning Skills

College forces you to plan. The syllabus gives you a whole semester or quarter to look at on the first day of class or on the first day it's posted on the school's Web page.

After recovering from the shock of how many books you'll need and how many reports or projects you'll have to do, you will make a plan, or should make a plan. When you see the date that midterms occur, you will realize not to plan an overnight camping trip or a bicycle weekend at the same time.

To fail to plan is to plan to fail. A familiar axiom in corporate offices and political campaigns, the need to plan becomes immediately obvious to college students. For some in technical specialties, such as engineering and computer science, there is little space for electives outside the specialty. Unfortunately, some students plan their courses up to graduation and have no connection to how the degree will fit in with their future life. A leftover impression from early days is that a college degree will somehow confer upon an individual a passport to life and that graduation itself is the goal.

You must develop planning skills in college and incorporate these skills into your college activities and life. The students who do not learn these skills are easy to spot: they drop out. Safe to say that if you have gotten to college, decided on a major, pursued it, and graduated, you have achieved some expertise in planning.

Accountability

Many upper-level courses in college today involve team projects. The team is judged as a whole, and the team members each receive the same grade. At the team's first meeting it quickly becomes apparent which team members will not be willing to pull their load. Usually the other team members put up with this and fill in the gap. The instructor leaves the discipline of the team to team members. Figuring out how to motivate the noncontributing member is part of the work of being on a team.

The benefit of these team projects is to show students how things occur in the "real" world. Students on the team who shun accountability incur hostility and animosity from other team members. Your team project experience will give you "team steam" in your career.

Perceptivity

Observing and perceiving people, events, speeches, groups, and interactions form an important part of the college experience. Kiosks and bulletin boards inform students daily of opportunities to hear guest speakers and to attend forums, concerts, debates, athletic events, and symposiums. Through this vast exposure on campus, you will have the opportunity to weigh different viewpoints, explore those differences, and increase your ability to perceive. Besides the vast public exposure, students hear the voices of professors offering views they may have never previously considered.

Tolerance

A diverse workforce is essential for the United States to remain competitive in the world. Students who have been raised in urban, suburban, or rural ghettos in which everyone is the same racially, economically, and religiously will be at a disadvantage in preparing for the future. Bringing people of different backgrounds together to be productive adds to the richness of the whole.

Most colleges try to maintain a diverse population in their acceptance process but frequently, upon graduation, students are shocked culturally with the attitudes and customs of the workforce they are asked to manage or collaborate with.

At college, seeking out people who are different from you will round out your education. Foreign students have much to add to your knowledge of the world. They might tell you, for instance, that, in their country, a man is allowed to have two wives and families if he can support both financially. Or that in their country there is no set schedule for mail to arrive; it might come every four days and then not again for a few weeks. American students benefit from knowing that countries vary enormously in their ways of interacting and living.

Coping Skills

With all the ups and downs of life on campus, coping skills prepare you to meet problems with confidence. The computer loses the grades, the adviser forgot to tell you about a course you need for graduation, the instructor didn't mention that he wanted MLA documentation on the research paper and you have to completely redo the citations. These events are good because they teach you how to cope. The skills you learn—politeness, patience, investigation of other ways to accomplish your task—will enrich your life on the outside. Knowing how to cope, no matter what happens, is a fundamental skill to learn on campus. Most people won't graduate without it.

Initiative and Leadership Skills

You need to overcome the tendency to hesitate too long while you're thinking of reasons you shouldn't move ahead. Initiative and leadership skills mean acknowledging that mistakes will be made which is better than regretting chances you didn't take. Initiative means going for it, catching the train, jumping on the bandwagon, following the calliope. In the words of Nike, it means, "Just Do It."

Perseverance

"There are doers and there are stewers," is a saying former Senator Bob Dole learned from his father in Kansas. The lesson he learned at home helped him through massive injuries suffered in World War II that eliminated the hope he had of being a surgeon and started him on the path to becoming a senator.

War talk aside, working toward a degree does prove whether you have the stamina to finish a job you started. Employers want to know that you can jump through the hoops that college demands. In some classes the instructor won't speak English, in others you won't be able to decipher what is being written on the board or shown on the overhead projector. You will face final exams that cover too much material for anyone's brain capacity. You will have poor teachers who would rather not spend time in the classroom and don't keep office hours.

Surely, these situations are not as bad as Dole's having his body severely injured in wartime Italy and enduring three years of painful rehabilitation to recover. But sometimes college will feel awful. That's where this skill of perseverance will come in.

How will you know if you have developed this skill in college? You will receive a piece of paper called a diploma that attests to your skill of perseverance. With this piece of paper you will become a college graduate. This tells people that you have achieved a level of perseverance, no matter how long it has taken. For this, you deserve congratulations.

CHAPTER 9

LEARNING FROM OTHERS: REAL PEOPLE TALK ABOUT THEIR MAJORS

Philosophies differ on what a college education should be. Having a good time for four years is a popular notion. Others, witnessing tough economic readjustment over the past few years, believe college should prepare you for a job. The traditional belief is that college is a time to grow, to broaden your awareness. In the following comments, many former students offer their opinions on what a major means and how the one they chose has affected their lives.

Jamie Wirt, Roosevelt University
Majors: Music, History

Music is my area of life. I work in music and play in music. I fell into a history major by taking many history courses, and by just taking a

155

few more, I earned a major. I did, although, enjoy the classes and even received an award in history.

My music major gave me several skills that relate directly to my current job(s), such as my aural and voice training in discerning pitch and musical nuance. I also learned valuable tools that I use as a producer, things like song structure and harmonic content. Some skills, like intensive computer and technical skills, I gained through experience in the studio.

If I had it to do all over again, I would have chosen a school where the composition teachers would have done more to lead me in interesting and pertinent directions.

The best advice I can give is to get a degree in a well-rounded area, (i.e., Bachelor of Arts). Don't worry so much about job skills as related to a major; just get a general degree to open your mind to what life has to offer, and then you can proceed from there.

Sam Saad III, University of Nebraska
Major: Marketing. Minor: Political Science

I am currently an attorney advisor for the Department of Labor. I was influenced to major in marketing by my parents and guidance counselors, and learned about the principles of marketing like supply chain management, vertical integration, etc. The only thing I learned from my major that has any effect on my work today is how to use Power-Point. I took a business law course as part of the program I was in, loved the subject matter and aced it without even trying. It was just basic contract law, but I was hooked. I went to law school and discovered a whole other world of thinking that business school never introduced me to. If I could go back, I would not major in marketing because I had very little interest in it. I just did what I was told and had no real interest in the classes, even though I did well in them. Looking back I would like to have been an engineering major, and I would have taken all philosophy and science classes.

When you get to college, take lots of diverse classes and don't let the university pigeonhole you into a program from the start. Try everything! Take literature, science, philosophy, everything. When you have an "ah ha!" moment, latch on to it and follow that path—it will probably be the right one. I had mine in my business law class, so I checked out philosophy and logic, and I loved it. There was only one choice for me after that, and it was law school.

Scott Minafri, Glassboro State College
Major: Management Information Systems

I've always had a knack for computing, but I didn't want to be completely technical, like computer science. Management Information Systems (MIS) gave me an opportunity to be exposed to the management side of things as well as the technical. I'm a Network Manager and manage the Local Area Network and handle PC support for a company's finance division. This encompasses about 20 file servers, and about 450 users. I have three systems administrators working for me. The worst part of my job is the hours—they can sometimes be a little crazy. The best part is being able to work with the new technology immediately once it becomes available.

My major, unfortunately, does not relate much to my current job. MIS is a lot of theory, not practice. Being an MIS major helped with my managerial skills, but that's about it. The one thing that college was good for is that it taught me how to think. My job requires a strong aptitude for computer systems, the ability to be resourceful, and the ability to take initiative.

Daniel Dutile, University of Notre Dame
Major: Business Administration/Finance

It really was a process of elimination for me. I knew I wanted something in business. Marketing, management and accounting were not really to my liking, however. Finance was left as the choice offering me enough business focus, with enough flexibility of curriculum.

As an equity portfolio manager, I am responsible for deciding where a portion of a large corporate retirement plan's assets should be invested. The best part of my job is making sense of the actions of the stock markets around the world. The worst part is dealing with the frustration when the stock markets' movements defy analysis.

As a finance major, I was exposed to the basic theories that tend to govern financial markets. I utilize this knowledge to analyze the markets in which we invest. My job requires skills in financial analysis, decision-making, communication of ideas, and personnel management.

I underestimated the importance of accounting skills in my career and in financial analysis in general. If I had it to do all over again, I would improve these skills. The best advice I can give students is to choose a major that you enjoy. Competence will show itself in whatever major is chosen. The future will then take care of itself.

Deborah Prince, University of Iowa
Major: Therapeutic Recreation

As a Recreational Therapist I assess patients according to their disabilities and interests, adapt activities that enable them to do the things they want to do and help them as much as possible. The best part of my job is working and getting to know each patient on an individual basis. The worst is the same as the best—knowing and caring about the patients. It's hard not to get personally involved, and when they leave or pass away, it is very difficult.

My major relates exactly to what I do now. I learned how to document and assess patients and disabilities in school. My job requires the ability to relate to people who are sick, and strong documentation skills.

Honestly, I wouldn't change a thing if I had to go back. I feel being able to do something for someone else is very rewarding. I would advise students to choose a field that you know you can wake up in the morning and be enthusiastic about. Recreational Therapy allows me to do just that.

Gregory Fung, Harvard College
Major: Biochemistry

I chose this major because when I first entered college, I felt fairly certain that I would either go into medicine or bio-medical research. As far as I could tell, this major provided the best opportunities for both of those fields.

In my first year after college I worked with urban squatters in the Philippines. Then I became a volunteer staff worker for InterVarsity Christian Fellowship. This job consists of helping lead a college Christian fellowship, including leading Bible Studies, teaching during leadership training times, organizing retreats and other events, pastoring students, and other related activities.

The best part of the job is being able to take part, see, and contribute to students' spiritual, mental, and emotional growth. The worst part is in feeling (and note that these feelings are not necessarily true) that the job is pointless, unproductive, hurtful to my future, and degrading.

My college major has almost nothing to do with what I do now, except that I can relate well with students who are in the same biochemistry or pre-med track that I was on.

My job requires (in order of importance): counseling skills, teaching skills, leadership/administration, good speaking or musical skills, depending on the specific ministry one is in.

If I could do it all over again, I would not major in biochemistry. I would probably have done something in the social sciences like sociology, psychology, or anthropology. I may even have gone the philosophy route. The core of the choice would be to go for a broader and more socially relevant major, rather than a narrower and skill-focused field (assuming that I would know that I would not end up in medicine).

I would say than you need not rush to make a decision concerning a major, or feel like you need to stick to the decision once made. I would also say that certain "career" majors such as biology should only be chosen if you think that you could do nothing else. Even if you end up going into biology, you can wait to fulfill the major requirements and take other classes so you don't lose out on the unique things a college education can offer.

Alexandra Wray, Cornell University
Majors: Art, Architecture

Cornell offered a five-year accredited program that allowed me to obtain a bachelor's degree in architecture, as opposed to simply majoring in the field. It is a professional degree and the training for architecture is well-rounded, so even had I chosen not to be an architect, I still received a great education.

I am currently licensed as an architect and work in a downtown Chicago firm. I have been working in the field for almost nine years. While my level of responsibility has increased, many tasks and skills carry through the years. Working to assist a team, building models, and doing presentation drawings comprised tasks in the early years of my career. Now, I may do those tasks as well as consultant management, client meetings, design, and technical review. My job requires neatness and careful thought, for example when producing an architectural model, I must be quick yet construct the model as perfectly as possible. Rendering drawings, AutoCAD, three-dimensional thought are also very important skills.

One of the most valuable skills of all is the ability to work well with other people. Over the years I have met the most interesting, talented, and varied group of people. The perspective I have gained by working with others is a major part of my professional development.

The creativity and variation of day-to-day activities is one of the best aspects of the profession. This profession is, however, stressful and it takes careful time management to not let it invade one's personal life. Deadlines seem to always appear just when they're most unwanted!

Lara Rhame, Bates College
Major: Economics

It was the end of my sophomore year, and I needed to choose. So I thought economics or psychology were the best mix of practical and interesting, and I went to talk to professors in each department. The econ professors were much more impressive. I was taking both at the time, and I really liked economics better.

As a risk manager I evaluate portfolio, credit and market risk on the trading floor at one of the big trading firms. The best part of my job is learning every day about the markets and being in the center of the international financial world. The worst are the egocentric, mean, self-centered, ultra-capitalistic traders and salespeople you have to deal with.

My major doesn't relate especially well to my job, except for the way economic factors could influence the market. But they are definitely in the same arena, with a lot of overlapping (especially the math classes I had to take).

My job requires quick thinking, the gift of gab, the ability to learn on the fly, computer and financial skills, statistics and math skills.

I am a fan of liberal arts, but I was careful to choose a major I thought would be practical. For example, I was very interested in Japanese art and religions, and thought about double majoring in Asian culture. In the end, it would have been overkill. But now I have it as a hobby, and still follow it passionately. This is not to say to major in something you abhor, just for practical reasons, but really think it through. There is a difference between thinking something is cool and wanting to center your college experience around it.

Margaret Wuebbels, Southern Methodist University
Majors: Psychology, History. Minor: Women's Studies

I was interested in becoming a psychologist at one point, I also had an interest in law and I thought history would be helpful, as would psychology. I am a trial lawyer and a public defender. I represent criminally indigent people. The best part of my job is being in court. The worst is the frustration with "the system."

My majors both required lots of writing. My background in psychology is helpful in selecting juries and dealing with people: other attorneys, reluctant witnesses, and clients. History gave me an overall intellectual view of law in American history. My job requires the ability to speak in public, and argue a case in court. It also demands the ability to negotiate and write clearly.

I would do nothing differently if given the chance. I waited three semesters to pick a major and really explored my options. Shop around. Study something you enjoy because you'll never get to do it again.

Natalie Melnik, University of Pittsburgh
Major: Sociology. Minor: French

I am an International Sales Coordinator for a multi-national firm. I provide consultations and various sales support to the U.S.-based sales people at my company, as well as the foreign. The best part of my job is working with people. The worst part of my job is working with people.

My major helped me develop people skills, an understanding of the psychology of the business environment, statistics skills, demography, intercultural understanding, and computer skills. My job requires all of these skills, plus communications skills and a mentality to get the job done.

I would not change a thing. I still love my major. I was never disappointed once in four years. It's very multi-faceted. I would advise students to match their genuine interests with the college programs and course offerings.

Sarah Kennedy, Loyola University
Major: Sociology. Minor: Social Work

I originally chose social work as a major, but switched because it only focused on the person as the problem and not necessarily the system. Sociology focused more on the system and how to create change in this area. I enjoyed sociology much more.

I am the Associate Director for a non-profit agency working with teenagers. We have programs in public schools and the surrounding communities of the specific schools. The programs use peer-to-peer interventions to help stop violence. It is an agency committed to work-ing with at-risk economically poor young adults to motivate them into becoming more responsible. The best part of the job, working with teens, is also the most challenging, but I do enjoy it. The worst is see-ing peer pressure and gangs and to deal with death, abuse, neglect, and lack of values.

I'm in the social service field, so my major has helped me under-stand more systematically what's going on. For example, I must look at one teen's behavior and discover why she is acting this way. Sociol-ogy helped me to do this. Someone who is abused may act out in many ways, or someone who is very overweight may have had many prob-lems in his past.

We must look at people's behavior, but don't judge, accept it and challenge them to become more positive. My job requires me to work with people; it requires skills of facilitating, conflict management, and the ability to implement change.

Gemma Smith, Texas Christian University
Major: Radio, TV & Film. Minor: Psychology

I chose my major for the most frivolous of reasons. I knew I wanted to be in communications, and there was this multiple choice question my first day of college. It said: 1) Journalism, 2) Advertising, or 3) Radio, TV & Film. Check one. So I checked Radio, TV & Film because I fig-ured I might as well enjoy myself for the next four years. And I did.

I am an Associate Producer right now for two TV series on a cable network. I write, organize information, coordinate crews, manage budgets, and try to choose great shots when editing shows. The best part of my job is the excitement of the set and being on location. The tremendous challenge of creativity: something out of nothing. And the diversity of projects. The worst is the challenge of creativity: some-thing great out of nothing. And the long hours.

My major relates to what I do in mostly superficial ways. Spending time in college learning the basics of production is silly in retrospect because I learned all my real production skills on the job. Technology changes so fast that the equipment I used in college just nine years ago is totally antiquated. Some classes on theory and the social impact and responsibility of the media were valuable to me in developing my per-spective. As a whole, I think a journalism or English major would have been more beneficial to me because being a good writer is very important in television (although it might be hard to believe sometimes).

My job requires enthusiasm, endurance, written communication skills, and oral communication skills. In TV you must be able to explain your idea of shots and visual images to a lot of people. Being able to accurately communicate your vision for a project is critical. The inability to do this can cost you thousands of dollars and days of shooting.

If I had it to do all over again, I would concentrate more on my writing skills. I would also take more speech classes to learn to project and to organize my thoughts. I would still minor in psychology, because understanding where people are coming from and their basic motivations is helpful no matter what you do. I sometimes wonder if my major would have been totally useless if I hadn't pursued a career in TV. But, I know a lot of people with the same degree doing various unrelated things, and they are very successful. I think I made the right choice because I really enjoyed the classes in college and I really enjoy my work now.

Joe Sifferman, Texas A & M University
Major: Industrial Engineering

I chose an engineering degree for several reasons not necessarily related to the specific content of the fields of study. An engineering degree would allow me to sharpen and refine my problem solving abilities, it would allow me more freedom for job and career selection in the future, and it would be a challenge. I originally chose bioengineering because I had entertained thoughts of pursuing a career in the medical field. I ended up going into industrial engineering because it's a good all-around engineering degree. It has more emphasis on business concepts than other engineering disciplines. I.E. also provides a strong background in economic and statistical analysis.

I am currently an Analyst for Information Technology for a management consulting firm. The best part of my job is the variety of work and the work environment. There are tremendous opportunities for learning, travel, and a potential for a future. The worst part is the long hours (50–60 hours a week). My job requires analytical thinking, problem solving, the ability to learn and adapt, and computer skills. I gained all of these skills through my majors. I would change nothing if given the opportunity.

The best advice I can give is choose something that interests you (that should be obvious), but that also provides the greatest potential (not necessarily monetary) for you and your future. I submit that most people in industry do not use their specific collegiate education knowledge in their everyday work. Therefore, I believe the most important things to get out of school are how to learn, exposure to various fields of study, basic/core knowledge (writing skills, math/statistics skills, etc.), and exposure to diversity (cultures, ways of thinking, etc.).

Catherine Berghoff, Northern Arizona University
Major: Communications. Minor: Business

After I got my undergraduate degree, I realized I wanted to work with kids whose native language wasn't English. I've always enjoyed studying language, and education seemed to fit my needs. I'm an ESL teacher at the middle school level. I teach six ESL math and bilingual classes a day. I'm also department chair for ESL and math. The best part of my job: I love working with kids, presenting them with new information and getting them excited to learn. The worst is the paperwork, and there are never enough hours in the day.

My undergraduate degree doesn't relate, except with the people skills I acquired. My master's degree relates because it's so specific—linguistics and working with children learning two languages, how to best teach them, and assess them as well. My job requires the skills of planning, organization, patience, and people skills (you have to be approachable).

If I could do it all over again, I would have studied education in my undergraduate years and listened more to myself and what I wanted to do as opposed to peers and family pressure to pursue a career that didn't really suit me.

David Shroder, Illinois Institute of Technology
Major: Architecture. Minor: Computer Science

I chose this major because I liked the feeling of designing and building something that I could point to and say, "I built that." There is a satisfaction there that cannot be found in many things these days.

I am the Manager of Software Development for a company that builds video display systems for airlines and airports around the world. I design and write the software that communicates the changes for various flight information to the displays as well as directing the activities of several other programmers. The best part of my job is that I get to be involved in the day-to-day running of a small company, and to see a product grow from an idea to hardware running at a customer's site. The worst are the emergencies. Our customers expect us to be available 24 hours a day, seven days a week. It can be a drain sometimes, especially with a very small group like we have.

Architecture taught me how to build very large things. This can be translated to the building of computer systems and products. Of all the things I learned in school, the ability to think "in the large" was probably the most useful. My job requires creativity, flexibility, analytical thinking, and patience.

In many ways, my career to this point has not been anything like I expected when I started college. However, I've been fortunate in being able to use the skills I developed there. Maybe not in the way I expected, but all things considered I would only change decisions I made about jobs, not about college, if given the chance.

My advice to students is to find something that will keep you interested and learning after you leave college. If what you know gets you a job, but you don't enjoy it, there isn't much point to it no matter how much money you make.

Joseph Chin, Wesleyan University
Major: College of Social Studies

I chose the College of Social Studies (CSS) because it provides a unique approach to learning that complements my interests perfectly. Coming out of high school, I knew that I was interested in government and foresaw myself in some form of a political science program. However, upon arriving at Wesleyan I discovered the CSS and instantly fell in love. CSS is an interdisciplinary program consisting of government, economics, history, and philosophy. It's a three-year major, beginning in the sophomore year. To enroll, students must submit an application to the college and participate in an interview during the spring semester of their freshman year.

CSS is fondly known as the College of Suicidal Sophomores by Wesleyan students due to its infamous workload. It was this prestigious and daunting reputation that first drew my attention. Upon further investigation I decided that the interdisciplinary approach to learning in the social sciences was ideal. I applied, and luckily, was admitted. CSS demands first and foremost a willingness to work. "Any means necessary" is the motto of a CSS major the night before a paper is due. CSS is also grounded in discussion and discourse. Classes are intentionally limited to 10–20 students. Therefore, students should be willing to engage one another in intellectual dialogue. Finally, CSS demands at least basic writing skills. But regardless of one's training or disposition to writing, at the end of the three years in CSS, one's writing skills invariably improve.

Juniors and seniors enjoy a significant increase in autonomy in choosing classes and have virtually free license to write their honors thesis on any topic they wish, as long as it falls under one of the four broad disciplines of CSS. College tutors have also made a concerted effort to integrate feminist theory into their classes.

David Simmons, Bowdoin College
Majors: German, Religion

I feel that I didn't really "choose" these majors; the majors chose me. In my sophomore year in high school my family hosted an exchange student from Germany, and I began to study German; after graduating from high school I spent a year with that student and his family in northern Germany. Although I had taken two years in high school, I could not speak much German at all when I first arrived, but over the course of the year I became quite fluent. When I matriculated at Bowdoin, the German department placed me in a 300-level German literature course, which required reading literature and writing analytical papers in German. I skipped over the beginning and intermediate courses, which do not count toward the major. Since the very first class I took in German counted toward the major, it was clear that it would be one of my majors.

I was not entirely satisfied with a single major, however; German almost seemed to be cheating since I already spoke the language. In my first year, I took introductory courses in anthropology, sociology, and religion. Religion 101 was by far the most exciting of these. It was a well-designed course, a little offbeat, and the professor was excellent. The following semester I signed up for a First-Year Seminar on the Book of Job. I was amazed by this seminar and did quite well. The professor, who taught courses in Judaism, Christianity, and Bible, persuaded me in the most positive terms to continue with religion.

The most difficult part of the German major was producing original, creative thought in a second language and communicating it both orally and in writing. For religion, it is being able to identify and understand religious behavior in cultures that are often extravagantly different from our own, and writing about religious patterns and activity in relationship to broader cultural contexts without sounding like a flake.

Religion demands open-mindedness and sensitivity, prerequisites for studying religions that sometimes seem bizarre, and an ability to place details into a larger picture that explains how humans relate to their universe in a religious metaphor. The ability to analyze shrewdly and write clearly is also essential.

People assume that all religion majors are theologians with plans for the ministry, which is absurdly untrue. Sometimes people become confessional around us and feel it necessary to explain that they haven't gone to church recently or are lapsed Catholics, or secular Jews, or whatever. We have to be very patient as we explain that the study of religion is not restricted to either Christianity or God. Religion majors are probably the most diverse group of individuals with different backgrounds and interests that I can think of, but sadly the stereotype is perpetuated by people who are stuck in a religious rut.

My personal feeling is that students are drawn to the study of religion because they have had some moment of "enlightenment" in which they came to question what they had been taught about religion by their own traditions. Many of them feel marginalized by the major traditions, and seek meaningful alternatives. Nearly all of them, I believe, have some kind of personal commitment to a certain area of religious expression that becomes the focus of their studies.

Chris Kalwett, Northern Illinois University
Major: Engineering Technology

I chose my major because it is more "hands-on" than mechanical or electrical engineering. In my job as a manufacturing engineer I find ways to improve productivity, efficiency, quality, ergonomics, and overall manufacturing. My job is most satisfying because many of the things I improve are noticeable soon after implementation.

There are a wide variety of skills that help me every day. They include an overall knowledge of modern manufacturing principles, solid understanding of mechanics, machines, and tooling, and computer proficiency—most modern machinery is computer controlled. Lastly, despite having a technical job, communication skills are essential. My major relates almost 100 percent to what I do now. Many of the principles and practices I learned relate to everyday projects.

Ceres Chua, Emory University
Majors: Biology, Chemistry

Ever since I took my first biology class in high school, I knew that biology was a subject I wanted to pursue. After taking additional courses in college, it became very clear to me that it was what I wanted to do. As for my chemistry major, I decided to study it out of convenience. I only needed to take two more classes after all of the chemistry that satisfied biology prerequisites to complete the major.

There is nothing in particular that's hard about my biology major, except that the subject is too dynamic. It is an ever-changing field, so one is required to keep up with it, especially when engaged in research. The hardest part about my chemistry major is physical chemistry. It is impossible to understand.

Lisa Huffhines, University of Texas at Arlington
Major: Nursing

I chose nursing for its flexibility and versatility—flexible work hours, and versatile positions, locations, and opportunities for advancement. It is a career, not a job. Nursing changes roles as healthcare changes routes of delivery.

The hardest part of studying nursing is the many hours put into book work as well as clinical hours. The full-time student (12–15 hrs) will be busy Monday through Friday, 8:00 a.m. to 5:00 p.m. That makes it difficult to work much.

Jennifer Shaw, University of Illinois at Chicago
Major: English

I went to a college preparatory high school at which we were strongly encouraged to have a major chosen as early as junior year. Having little information at hand, and certainly not enough life experience, I chose Occupational Therapy at the ripe age of seventeen. UIC was the only school in the state with the program, so that's where I went.

The first year was just general education, a lot of psychology, some biology. But when it came time to register for my sophomore year— the year I would need two consecutive anatomy classes— I found the one and only anatomy class of 500 seats was closed. Oh well, I thought, I guess I'll have to take it next year. But the next year, it was closed, and I wondered why in the world at such a big school (and one with so many medical professions, for that matter) would they offer only one anatomy class per semester? I assumed my advisor could somehow overenroll me, so I went to see him, totally unprepared for the reaming I was to receive regarding my grades. He told me in no uncertain terms that "B"s and "C"s are not acceptable, and I need not bother applying to the OT program, because I would not be accepted. He even went on to suggest that I see a counselor if I'd been having any personal problems. I sat there, paralyzed, wondering if I would cry first or throw a punch his way for even suggesting that I had problems. I didn't say a word; I just nodded when he told me to change my major.

Don't get me wrong, I will always despise that man for treating me the way he did, but he was right. The OT program wasn't for me. Not with those grades. The truth was, I had made that choice too early, and knew nothing about it. So I took a serious look at what I had been doing in school, and how I had been doing, when I noticed a peculiar pattern. I had nearly flunked all tests, and aced all papers. Sure, it evened out to a nice, round "C," but that was when I realized that I had a talent for writing. Yes, I thought. Why not just write? So I quickly changed my major to English, and began getting "A"s and the occasional "B" (in electives in other disciplines, of course).

There's no doubt in my mind that I made the right decision. I have one huge advantage over all other Liberal Arts and Sciences graduates: I can write. And I don't mean just term papers or poetry or fiction or non-fiction. Writing is so much more than that. It's quick comprehension, it's a love of words, it's creativity. Sure, there are stereotypes of English majors. But they don't bother me as much as the questions I've answered a million times or more. "What are you going to do with an English degree?" "So you're going to teach?" And I swear, I've heard this one at least five times, "How can you major in your own native language?" Over the years you manage to come up with some snappy comebacks. It's all part of belonging to that "useless" major.

The best advice I can give students is to not declare anything for the first two years unless you absolutely have to. If you look at any college handbook, the general requirements are pretty much the same anywhere you go, so you can see what you like and fulfill those requirements at the same time. Neat trick, huh? Oh, and of course, pick something that interests you (although I don't know many people who pick things that don't interest them).

And be honest with yourself. If you're not doing so well in what you picked, ask yourself if you really wanted to do it in the first place. If it is, then you better get to work, and if not, then you have to find out what you can do. Sometimes change is good.

Tracey Holloway, Brown University
Major: Applied Mathematics

When I began college, I thought I would major in History or Political Science. The rather drastic switch to Applied Math occurred through a series of trials and errors. First semester, I took two classes in the humanities/social sciences and two in math/physical sciences. The science classes were primarily to keep open the pre-med option, which was the most "sciency" career I'd considered. However, I loved first year chemistry and enjoyed math more than I ever had in high school.

Many of my friends that first year planned on majoring in science, and I began to consider this idea as well. After some thought, I decided to try engineering, which seemed to combine creativity and science in the design process. One semester of that program, however, turned me off to engineering as my science field of choice. (I felt it was too dry, and much less creative than other branches of science, contrary to my initial hope. In retrospect, I think that engineering actually could be quite enjoyable, but that initial course did not succeed in convincing me at the time.) Sophomore year, I took a course in Linear Algebra, which I loved, and it convinced me that higher mathematics offered my desired blend of creativity and problem-solving. Concurrently, I took an economics class, which I also liked, and decided that by majoring in applied mathematics, I could pursue both math and economics. Although I ended up focusing on fluid dynamics (an active research area in the applied math department) rather than economics in later years of college, the choice to major in applied math was motivated by a desire to combine economics with mathematics.

My advice to those choosing a major is to give a lot of thought to what would make you really happy and excited to do in the long run, and try to learn how the career you want ties back into classes you could take. Then, think of what other careers this major would prepare you for if you change your mind or can't get your ideal position. Although there are not that many astronauts in the world, preparing for a "dream job" like that would prepare you for other, related jobs, whether in the space program, or as a scientific researcher, or as a pilot, or as a science teacher. I'd say, prepare for your ultimate job, but try to keep other options open as long as possible.

Julie Ann Perschbacher, Stanford University
Majors: Classics, History

Today I work as a Judicial Clerk for a Federal District Court Judge, where I research information, write memos for the judge, and give advice on motions filed in court. Throughout college I considered teaching (history) or grad school (classics). Eventually during my senior year I decided that I would really like to attend law school. I don't know if high schoolers are aware of this, but there are no prerequisites in terms of classes or majors for law school. In fact, there are too many political science majors going to law school so it is almost more interesting to schools if you major in something else. I even know biology majors in law school! Anyhow, I decided to move to Washington, DC, and work as a paralegal for a few years (again, no specific major was required) to make sure I wanted to go to law school, and eventually I did go to law school.

It was after law school that I decided to work as a Judicial Clerk for a judge for a year, but it's not only a temporary position. There are also permanent clerks. I will finish up this job in August and then go to a big law firm and become a boring lawyer. In college I immensely enjoyed my majors—I learned a lot and really enjoyed all the material. I chose my majors because I had a genuine interest in the subjects, and I would recommend that any student study what interests him or her the most. The jobs will follow.

Wai-Sinn Chan, Yale University
Major: Psychology

Freshman year I was considering 18 different majors (ok, five seriously). First semester it had narrowed down to five, second semester down to one. I really enjoyed Introductory Psych so I took more upper level courses, which led me to the major.

I really had no idea what I wanted to do in the future and based my decision on good classes and professors more than other more practical considerations, i.e., what are you going to do with that?! Psychology is a broad field so I could really dabble in my different interests.

Although a typical psych paper is very structured and has less room for creativity, I really learned how to write a solid APA (American Psychological Association) style paper. More creative papers such as experiment proposals and my senior essay were good exercises in problem solving. These are skills useful for many jobs in market research. I will especially need to be able to put problem solving and writing skills to use. Today I work for an advertising agency and use my research, analytical, and writing skills.

If I had it to do all over again, I would try to focus more within the major into more directly related fields like marketing or into graduate school. I enjoyed the freedom of the major but would have preferred more of a focus. I would also have considered double majoring more seriously. Also, taking interdisciplinary courses such as sociology and education was also valuable.

Scott Facher, Dartmouth College
Major: Theater

I chose Theater because I loved reading plays. I found myself drawn to certain professors in these departments. But, mostly, when it was time to choose a major my passions were outside the classroom. My love for acting had started to grow. I loved to play the violin. I loved my friends in college. In college there were a million things I wanted to be doing when I wasn't in class. Reading assignments weren't usually among them. But there were moments reading a play or novel where I wouldn't have wanted to be anywhere else.

I've called myself an actor since graduation. I got my first paying job doing summer stock right out of college. The best part of my job is the acting, all of it. Rehearsing, an actor is like a psychologist or archeologist, exploring the human psyche, finding the connection between ourselves and others—an actor is also an archeologist of the human mind and spirit.

If I hadn't followed my passion for acting in college, I certainly wouldn't be doing it, or pursuing it, now. I chose to be an actor because it seemed and still seems the best way for me to get my voice out in the world.

Don't worry so much about "what will help you when you graduate." Maybe if you know early on that you have a passion for sciences or for economics, then focusing there could help you in your post-graduation plans. But, what a liberal arts education teaches you is how to learn and how to think. So, major in what you are passionate about.

Jessica M. Schindhelm, Bowdoin College
Major: Women's Studies

I think the hardest part of my major is defending it to others. People are always asking me, "What can you do with a Women's Studies Major?" I usually reply with something like, "What can you do with a Liberal Arts degree regardless of the major?" I mean today's job market really doesn't cater to those who don't have work experience or a graduate degree.

My major more fits into my attitude than my career. It has given me an outlook on life that allows me to question the standards and perhaps to open some closed minds. Of course there are stereotypical images with this major as with every major. I think that the most harmful of these is the "angry young woman" or "lesbian." I personally don't mind being called either because if I don't validate people's claims, then they are no longer harmful.

Jason Black, Michigan State University
Major: Urban Forestry

I originally went to the University of Oklahoma to major in Meteorology. I came to that decision because even as a young boy I would stay up late to watch the extended forecast on the late news. I was fascinated by the extremes, cold, hot, but most of all big storms (snow, tornadoes, etc.). Unfortunately, after two years of school I realized that I just did not have the mathematical skills to proceed through the program. After that I was at a total loss as to what my major should be. After three or four weeks and at my father's urging, I gave advertising a try. My father, his new wife and all their friends were in the advertising field, and I had grown up all around it. Unfortunately, that was disastrous.

I decided to quit school and work where I had the previous summers for the Streets/ Forestry Department doing tree trimming, planting, and removals. After working there for one and a half years I realized that forestry, particularly urban forestry, was for me. I felt rather stupid that it had taken me this long to realize this because as a small boy I was always trimming the trees and shrubs in the neighborhood as well as at my relatives when we went to visit. I chose urban forestry because I couldn't imagine being on a mountaintop out West in a national park. The city was too important a part of me to move away from. I also realized how important the environment was to me, not only maintaining it but improving and protecting it from outside interests but also from the natural pests and dangers that threaten our nation's forests.

Because urban foresters generally work for a city or state government, much more of their time is spent dealing with the public. Public Relations courses are required in the curriculum.

The advice I'd give is you shouldn't cave in to any pressures your friends or family might put on you. Don't feel that you must know what you want to major in immediately upon enrollment in college. You'll be much happier in life if you stay true to your heart and do what makes you happy.

Whitney Cassell, University of South Carolina
Major: Hotel/Restaurant/Tourism Administration

I currently work at a Presbyterian School as a Pre-school Teacher and as Assistant Director for Admission. I majored in Hotel Administration because my parents thought it would be a good fit for me. It was a very fun major in college, and very useful—it taught me customer service skills that are helpful in all jobs, like a strong work ethic, good communication, and knowing how to sell myself.

If I could go back, I would have been an education major since the profession of teaching fits me better. For my current position I am enrolled in an alternative teacher certification program that takes about 1.5 years and involves university classes. Teaching is a much more gratifying job because I feel like I am truly making a difference when I am teaching.

Bree Andrews, University of California, San Diego
Major: Biology. Minor: Sociology

I work as a Physician and Neonatology Fellow at the University of Chicago. My 55-to-70-hour work week includes clinical work coordinating and providing intensive care for 65 babies. I also develop lab research with the help of a mentor. Every sixth night I am on call, meaning I stay overnight at the hospital.

I majored in Biology because I wanted preparation for medical school while in college. My major helped me think like a physiologist and lay the groundwork for both memorization and biologic processes that are important in medicine.

Choose a major that can help you stay enthused about your coursework. The best and most beneficial aspect of college for me was that I learned to work and study effectively. You will not do yourself any favors by "just getting by" in college. Beyond choosing a major, I benefited from living in a residential college that supported small honors symposiums that allowed me to interact with internationally known scientists and humanitarians. I also was a teaching assistant for Introduction to Biology. Many colleges offer opportunities for practical learning experiences such as internships, which help you learn skills in your field of interest.

Many college students do not know of the range of careers that exist in the work world. I have been surprised to find out that I could have done many jobs related to medicine without becoming a doctor. I would have benefited from spending more time getting help from a career counselor and talking to people more about the diversity of careers in medicine. I was idealistic when I started medical school, thinking I could work as hard as anyone else; however, I have discovered that this lifestyle is very taxing. I think my work is tremendously interesting but it comes at a price of an inflexible schedule and intense decision-making at work.

Eliza Jacobs, University of Pennsylvania
Major: Communication

Today I am a graduate student at Georgetown University, and I work as a Research Assistant at the Children's Digital Media Center, whose goal is to improve the digital media environment in which children live and learn through studying how interactive digital media experiences affect children's long-term social adjustment, academic achievement, and personal identity.

Throughout high school I worked on the school newspaper and had an internship with the Buffalo Bisons working in the public relations department, and that's what sparked my interest in Communication. The major seemed interesting and most relevant to the field I wanted to enter, so I pursued it and learned mostly about Media Theory and how the media can influence behavior. As I moved on to college, I realized that I was more interested in the theory and how communication affects behavior than in the practical part, such as journalism. My interest has led me to continued study in graduate school, and it has provided me with a very useful background in the work force.

Make sure you take a broad selection of classes before choosing your major so you can see what's out there; you never know what will spark an interest. Don't let your parents dictate your choice of major, either. Choose a field you like, and not necessarily one that you see as most practical in terms of job prospects.

Jason Schroeder, University of Wisconsin at Whitewater
Majors: Finance, Economics

Today I work as a Pricing Analyst for a large, nationwide, insurance company. I help to price insurance and to implement new insurance products in the western United States. I have always had an interest in math, the stock market, and how business works—how they operate and make money. When I got to college, I was particularly interested in managing my own income, which stemmed from investments and an Internet business, so I decided to major in Finance. During my sophomore year, as I learned more and more about how the economy works, I added an Economics major.

My college experience showed me how businesses operate, how they allocate resources to maximize shareholder value, and how different parts of the economy interact together. In my work, most of my peers majored in Mathematics, and have a hard time determining the best business decision. My background in Finance and Economics gives me an advantage by enabling me to assess what decisions are best for the company.

If you are going to work for a public company, it is an asset to be able to make decisions that are best for the business. Knowing how companies acquire, maintain, and use their resources is important to succeed. When choosing a major students should look at the possible jobs that someone with that major would go into. It is important that you select a major that will allow you to get a job that you would like to have for a significant portion of the rest of your life.

Jim McLaughlin, Amherst College
Major: Political Science

Today I am an attorney for a Washington, D.C., law firm that focuses on white-collar criminal defense. I conduct civil and criminal litigation on behalf of the firm's clients and represent those clients in court. I also research and draft briefs, supervise discovery, and take and defend depositions. I felt political science would be a good major to prepare myself for law school, and the political science courses I took early in my college career helped to guide me to it as my major. My major gave me an understanding of the major political thinkers from classical times into the twentieth century. I also developed an appreciation of the links between political theory and concrete policy choices. My major also improved my analytical and writing skills.

My cases often involve issues of public policy, so my background as a political science major gives me a useful perspective on that. Additionally, many legal concepts are closely related to philosophical notions of liberty, individual rights, property, the state, and so on. If I had it to do all over again, knowing what I know now, I would have majored in Classics or Literature, which interest me more, and would only have taken a handful of political science courses. You should follow your interests in your undergraduate career. Don't worry about impressing employers or graduate schools. Unless you plan to enter a scientific or technical field, your major does not have to be what you plan to do for the rest of your life. Do something you're passionate about, and if you enjoy it, the results will follow.

Amanda Lenhart, Amherst College
Majors: English, Anthropology

Today I am a Research Specialist at the Pew Internet & American Life Project (PIP). In my position I am responsible for conducting research on children, education and the Internet, the digital divide, content creation, online communications tools, and other topics. I follow each project from beginning to end—doing background research, conceptualizing the research question, writing the survey, analyzing the data, writing it into a report, organizing, planning and then conducting focus groups, and then releasing the study publicly, which includes doing my own public relations for print, radio and occasionally television interviews. I also manage projects conducted by others outside of

PIP. I am also responsible for managing all aspects of the Project website, PIP's main mouthpiece to the world.

I selected English and Anthropology as majors because I loved literature, and after taking an anthropology class in high school, I knew that I was intrigued by the way the discipline approached the world and that I wanted to learn more about it. I learned how to think critically, how to write well, how to approach a difficult document, how to create arguments, and how to think broadly and outside of my own culture and experiences. I learned to question my own assumptions, and to think before I speak. I learned the value of a good narrative—how good storytelling can be used in many different disciplines to teach, to engage, to inform or to entertain.

I think my majors have impacted the trajectory of my work—the variety and nature of the different jobs I've had and tried out since I graduated. Because my major wasn't pre-professional in any way, I tried out different jobs before landing in my current position. I've worked in publishing and journalism and advocacy, and each of those wasn't exactly right in ways that I only discovered when I worked in the fields. My majors didn't prepare me for that, but did give me the basic skills to do those jobs. They gave my a great underpinning for doing my job, which requires me to essentially do "anthropology on the Internet" and then to write up what I learn in a clear and accessible way—both skills that I learned directly through my majors.

JOBS FOR THE TWENTY-FIRST CENTURY

L ife without change would be borrrrinnnng! Careers have been anything but boring in the last few years with downsizing and delayering. The days of security with gold 50-year-service watches are gone, and the exciting challenge of many careers in a lifetime is here.

Choosing a major with the world of work in this state of transition is tricky, but as stated in earlier chapters, it's the skills you learn through the major that are important, not the major itself. The major has to be an area that interests you enough so that you want to study it for four or more years, and one that has meaning in your life. However, to blindly choose a major with no thought to its future application is foolhardy. So, what are the experts saying?

Who Knows Better Than Uncle Sam?

The main source of information on the future of the job market is the U.S. Department of Labor, Bureau of Labor Statistics (BLS) and its *Occupational Outlook Handbook,* which is available online and in most libraries. This government bureau bases its projections on U.S. Census Bureau information. In addition, information is gathered from trade associations, professional societies, unions, industrial organizations, and gov-

ernment agencies. Note that the government cannot guarantee that any
information it receives from these sources is 100 percent accurate.

Look in Your Own Backyard

While federal labor statistics provide information on specific industry
growth, part of the data may not apply to your particular region or the
region in which you hope to work and live someday. To find information specifically by state, look online for the State Occupational Information Coordinating Committee (SOICC), usually located in the state
capital. Finding and deciphering the information from the state is
tedious, but it will give you an idea of job forecasting in your state.

The Government's Crystal Ball

Looking ahead until the year 2012, the fastest growing positions for
graduates with a bachelor's degree will be:

Medical assistants
Network systems analysts and data communications analysts
Social and human service assistants
Physician assistants
Home health aides
Medical records technicians and health information technicians

From now until the year 2010, the fastest growth will occur in the
following fields:

INDUSTRY	PERCENT CHANGE
Management and public relations	42
Miscellaneous equipment rental and leasing	42
Miscellaneous business services	44
Water and sanitation	45
Warehousing and storage	45
Personnel supply services	49
Cable and pay television services	51
Health services, not elsewhere classified	57
Residential care	64
Computer and data processing services	86

Interesting Facts

The long-term shift from goods-producing to service-providing employment is expected to continue. Service-providing industries are expected to account for approximately 20.8 million of the 21.6 million new wage and salary jobs generated over the 2002–2012 period.

For all but 1 of the 50 highest-paying occupations, a college degree or higher is the most significant source of education or training. Air traffic controller is the only occupation of the 50 highest paying for which this is not the case.

Following are the employment sectors that will create the most new jobs between now and 2012:

Education and Health Services

This industry supersector is projected to grow faster (by 31.8 percent) and add more jobs than any other industry supersector. About one out of every four new jobs created in the U.S. economy will be in either the health care and social assistance or private educational services sectors.

Health care and social assistance—including private hospitals, nursing and residential care facilities, and individual and family services—will grow by 32.4 percent and add 4.4 million new jobs. Employment growth will be driven by increasing demand for health care and social assistance because of an aging population and longer life expectancies. Also, as more women enter the labor force, demand for child care services is expected to grow.

Private educational services will grow by 28.7 percent and add 759,000 new jobs through 2012. Rising student enrollments at all levels of education will create demand for educational services.

Professional and Business Services

Professional and business services will grow by 30.4 percent and add nearly 5 million new jobs. This industry supersector includes some of the fastest growing industries in the U.S. economy.

Employment in administrative and support and waste management and remediation services will grow by 37 percent and add 2.8 million new jobs to the economy by 2012. The fastest-growing industry in this sector will be employment services, which will grow by 54.3 percent and will contribute almost two-thirds of all new jobs in administrative and support and waste management and remediation services. Employment services rank among the fastest-growing industries in the nation and are expected to be among those that provide the most new jobs.

You can find some great graphs at www.bls.gov/oco/images/ ocotjc08.gif, which lists the professions that will create the most jobs between now and 2012. And www.bls.gov/oco/images/ocotjc07.gif lists the employment fields that are growing at the fastest rates, regardless of relative employment quantity.

Specific Job Information

Check out the jobs listed below. Maybe you haven't considered some of them, and one will pique your interest.

Accountants and Auditors

Employment of accountants and auditors is expected to grow about as fast as the average for all occupations through the year 2012.

Budget analysis will be a highly competitive field according to the 2002–2012 projections. Candidates with a master's degree should have the best job opportunities. Employment of budget analysts is expected to grow about as fast as the average for all occupations through the year 2012.

Human Resources Assistants

Employment of human resources assistants (employment interviewers) is expected to grow about as fast as the average for all occupations through the year 2012.

Financial Managers

Employment of financial managers is expected to grow about as fast as the average for all occupations through 2012.

Health Services Managers

Employment of medical and health services managers is expected to grow faster than the average for all occupations through 2012. Medical and health services managers must be familiar with management principles and practices. A master's degree in health services administration, long-term care administration, health sciences, public health, public administration, or business administration is the standard credential for most generalist positions in this field. However, a bachelor's degree is adequate for some entry-level positions in smaller facilities and at the departmental level within health care organizations.

Hotel Managers

Employment of hotel managers is expected to grow more slowly than the average for all occupations through 2012. Hotels increasingly emphasize specialized training. Postsecondary training in hotel or restaurant management is preferred for most hotel management positions, although a college liberal arts degree may be sufficient when coupled with related hotel experience.

Loan Counselors and Officers

Employment of loan counselors and officers is projected to grow about as fast as the average for all occupations through 2012. College graduates and those with banking, lending, or sales experience should have the best job prospects.

Management Analysts

Management analysts, often referred to as *management consultants* in private industry, analyze and propose ways to improve an organization's structure, efficiency, or profits. Despite projected rapid employment growth, keen competition is expected for jobs as management analysts. Job opportunities are expected to be best for those with a graduate degree, industry expertise, and a talent for sales and public relations. Employment of management analysts is expected to grow faster than the average for all occupations through 2012.

Advertising, Marketing, and Public Relations Managers

Employment of advertising, marketing, promotions, public relations, and sales managers is expected to grow faster than the average for all occupations through 2012.

Real Estate Managers

Employment of property, real estate, and community association managers is projected to grow about as fast as the average for all occupations through the year 2012. To businesses and investors, properly managed real estate is a potential source of income and profits, and, to homeowners, it is a way to preserve and enhance resale values. Property, real estate, and community association managers maintain and increase the value of real estate investments. Property and real estate managers oversee the performance of income-producing commercial or residential properties and ensure that real estate investments achieve their expected revenues. Community association managers manage the common property and services of condominiums, cooperatives, and planned communities through their homeowners' or community associations.

Engineering

Overall engineering employment is expected to grow more slowly than the average for all occupations over the 2002–2012 period. There are a large number of well-trained, often English-speaking engineers available in many countries who are willing to work at much lower salaries than are U.S. engineers. Many employers are increasing their use of engineering services performed in other countries. Despite this, overall job opportunities in engineering are expected to be good because the number of engineering graduates should be in rough balance with the number of job openings over this period.

Architects

Prospective architects (except landscape and naval) may face stiff competition for entry-level positions, especially if the number of architectural degrees awarded remains at current levels or increases. Employment of architects is projected to grow about as fast as the average for all occupations through 2012. Employment of landscape architects is expected to grow faster than the average for all occupations through the year 2012. Their expertise will be highly sought after in the planning and development of new residential, commercial, and other types of construction to meet the needs of a growing population.

Computer Gurus

Computer systems analysts, database administrators, and computer scientists are expected to be among the fastest-growing occupations through 2012. Employment of these computer specialists is expected to grow much faster than the average for all occupations as organizations continue to adopt and integrate increasingly sophisticated technologies. Increases in the number of these jobs will be driven by very rapid growth in computer system design and related services, which is projected to be one of the fastest-growing industries in the U.S. economy.

Employment of programmers is expected to grow about as fast as the average for all occupations through 2012.

Conservation Scientists

Employment of conservation scientists and foresters is expected to grow more slowly than the average for all occupations through 2012.

Chemists

Employment of chemists is expected to grow about as fast as the average for all occupations through 2012.

Lawyers

Employment of lawyers is expected to grow about as fast as the average for all occupations through 2012.

Paralegals and Legal Assistants

Jobs for paralegals and legal assistants are projected to grow faster than the average for all occupations through 2012. Despite projections of fast employment growth, competition for jobs should continue as many people seek to go into this profession; however, highly skilled, formally trained paralegals have excellent employment potential. Some employment growth stems from law firms and other employers with legal staffs increasingly hiring paralegals to lower the cost and increase the availability and efficiency of legal services. The majority of job openings for paralegals in the future will be new jobs created by employment growth, but additional job openings will arise as people leave the occupation.

Social Scientists

Anthropologists and archaeologists, geographers, and sociologists will experience average employment growth through 2012. However, employment of historians and political scientists will grow more slowly than average because these workers enjoy fewer opportunities outside of government and academic settings.

Economists

Employment of economists is expected to grow about as fast as the average for all occupations through 2012.

Social Workers

Employment of social workers is expected to grow faster than the average for all occupations through 2012. Competition for social worker jobs is stronger in cities, where demand for services often is highest and training programs for social workers are prevalent. However, opportunities should be good in rural areas, which often find it difficult to attract and retain qualified staff. By specialty, job prospects may be best for those social workers with a background in gerontology and substance abuse treatment.

Clergy

Job opportunities as Protestant ministers should be best for graduates of theological schools. The shortage of Roman Catholic priests is expected to continue, resulting in a very favorable job outlook through the year 2012. Job opportunities for rabbis are expected in all four major branches of Judaism through the year 2012. Rabbis willing to work in small, underserved communities should have the best prospects.

Special Education Teachers

Opportunities for jobs as adult literacy, remedial, and self-enrichment education teachers are expected to be favorable. Employment is expected to grow faster than the average for all occupations through 2012.

Teachers

Self-enrichment education teachers account for the largest proportion of jobs in these occupations. Significant employment growth is anticipated especially for English as a second language teachers, who will be needed by the increasing number of immigrants and other residents living in this country who need to learn, or enhance their skills in, English.

Job opportunities for teachers over the next 10 years will vary from good to excellent, depending on the locality, grade level, and subject taught.

College Instructors

Overall, employment of postsecondary teachers is expected to grow much faster than the average for all occupations through 2012. A significant proportion of these new jobs will be part-time positions. Postsecondary institutions are a major employer of workers holding doctoral degrees, and opportunities for Ph.D. recipients seeking jobs as postsecondary teachers are expected to be somewhat better than in previous decades. The number of earned doctorate degrees is projected to rise by only 4 percent over the 2002–2012 period.

Chiropractors

Employment of chiropractors is expected to grow faster than the average for all occupations through the year 2012 as consumer demand for alternative forms of health care grows.

Optometrists

Employment of optometrists is expected to grow about as fast as the average for all occupations through 2012.

Podiatrists

Employment of podiatrists is expected to grow about as fast as the average for all occupations through 2012.

Veterinarians

Pet doctors have a bright future. Very good opportunities are expected because the number of graduates from veterinary school is not expected to increase significantly over the 2002–2012 period. However, there is keen competition for admittance to veterinary school. Prospective veterinarians must graduate from a four-year program at an accredited college of veterinary medicine with a Doctor of Veterinary Medicine (D.V.M. or V.M.D.) degree and obtain a license to practice. Many of these colleges do not require a bachelor's degree for entrance, but all require a significant number of credit hours—ranging from 45 to 90 semester hours—at the undergraduate level.

Dieticians

Employment of dietitians is expected to grow about as fast as the average for all occupations through 2012.

Occupational Therapists

Employment of occupational therapists is expected to increase faster than the average for all occupations through 2012. The impact of proposed federal legislation imposing limits on reimbursement for therapy services might adversely affect the job market for occupational therapists in the near term. However, over the long run, the demand for occupational therapists should continue to rise as a result of growth in the number of individuals with disabilities or limited function who require therapy.

Pharmacists

Employment of pharmacists is expected to grow faster than the average for all occupations through the year 2012. Recent enrollments in pharmacy programs are rising as more students are attracted by high salaries and good job prospects. Despite this increase in enrollments, pharmacist jobs should still be more numerous than those seeking employment.

Physical Therapists

Employment of physical therapists is expected to grow faster than the average for all occupations through 2012.

Recreational Therapists

Overall employment of recreational therapists is expected to grow more slowly than the average for all occupations through the year 2012. Employment is expected to decline in hospitals as services shift to outpatient settings and employers emphasize cost containment. In nursing care facilities—the largest industry employing recreational therapists—employment will grow slightly faster than the occupation as a whole, as the number of older adults continues to grow.

Writers and Editors

Employment of writers and editors is expected to grow about as fast as the average for all occupations through the year 2012. The outlook for most writing and editing jobs is expected to be competitive, because many people with writing or journalism training are attracted to the occupation.

Designers

Overall employment of designers is expected to grow about as fast as the average for all occupations through the year 2012 as the economy expands and consumers, businesses, and manufacturers continue to rely on the services provided by designers. Designers will provide designs for ads, products, clothing, and every consumable item in our economy.

Actors, Producers, and Directors

Employment of actors, producers, and directors is expected to grow about as fast as the average for all occupations through 2012. Although a growing number of people will aspire to enter these professions, many will leave the field early because the work—when it is available—is hard, the hours are long, and the pay is low. Competition for jobs will be stiff, in part because the large number of highly trained and talented actors auditioning for roles generally exceeds the number of parts that become available. Only performers with the most stamina and talent will find regular employment.

Clinical Laboratory Workers

Employment of clinical laboratory workers is expected to grow about as fast as the average for all occupations through the year 2012, as the volume of laboratory tests increases with both population growth and the development of new types of tests.

Nuclear Medicine Technologists

Employment of nuclear medicine technologists is expected to grow faster than the average for all occupations through the year 2012. However, the number of openings each year will be relatively low because the occupation is small.

CHAPTER 11

FAMOUS PEOPLE AND THEIR MAJORS

Once people become famous, hardly anyone knows where they went to school, much less what they majored in. To show that professional success comes after a variety of majors and in many different packages, famous people and their majors are listed below. As you will read, many famous people became known in a field other than what they majored in.

Singer Art Garfunkel received his bachelor's degree from Columbia University in art history. His former musical partner Paul Simon holds an English degree from Queens College—City University of New York. Fellow Queens College alum Jerry Seinfeld majored in communications.

California Governor Arnold Schwarzenegger graduated from the University of Wisconsin—Superior. He majored in business and international economics. His wife, Maria Owings Shriver Schwarzenegger, author, newscaster, majored in American studies at Georgetown University. She wrote the book, *Ten Things I Wish I'd Known Before I Went Out into the Real World.*

Speaking of Californians, Academy-award-winning filmmaker Steven Spielberg majored in English at California State University at Long Beach. He made his first film, an eight-minute western, at age 12.

Garth Brooks earned his degree in advertising at Oklahoma State University. Jazz icon Herbie Hancock graduated from Grinnell College with majors in music and electrical engineering.

Jon Stewart played soccer and earned a degree in psychology from William and Mary College. The soccer team still presents an award called the "Liebo," named after Jon's birth name, Liebowitz, given to the clown/sweetheart of the team.

The Late Show host David Letterman received his bachelor's degree from Ball State University in telecommunications in 1969, and his rival *Tonight Show* host Jay Leno earned his speech therapy degree at Emerson College in Boston four years later in 1973.

Lifestyle celebrity Martha Stewart graduated from Barnard College in New York; her major was history and architectural history. TV and big-screen actor Tim Allen graduated from Western Michigan University with a degree in television production.

Human ecology is the sole major offered at the College of the Atlantic in Bar Harbor, Maine, and the major has served a number of its graduates including Nell Newman, of Newman's Own Organics; Chelie Pingree, the president of Common Cause; and Philip Kunhardt, author and filmmaker, who is a partner in the creation of the International Freedom Center in New York City. Nell's father, actor Paul Newman graduated from Kenyon College in 1949 with a degree in drama.

George W. Bush, the 43rd President, earned his degree in history from Yale University, and First Lady Laura Bush majored in education at Southern Methodist University. Bush's opponent in the 2004 presidential election, Senator John F. Kerry, also graduated from Yale, with a degree in political science. President George Herbert Walker Bush (the 41st President) graduated from Yale, too, with a degree in economics. President Bill Clinton graduated from Georgetown University with a degree in international affairs. His first lady and now U.S. senator, Hillary Rodham Clinton, as well as his Secretary of State, Madeleine Albright, both majored in political science at Wellesley College. Richard Nixon graduated from Whittier College in 1934 with a history major.

The first woman to sit on the U.S. Supreme Court, Sandra Day O'Connor, received her bachelor's degree in economics from Stanford University. Supreme Court Justice Clarence Thomas graduated from College of the Holy Cross in Massachusetts with a degree in English.

U.S. Senator Barack Obama graduated from Columbia University with a degree in political science, specializing in international relations.

Stewart Mott, founder of General Motors, received his mechanical engineering degree from Stevens Institute of Technology. Fellow Stevens alum, renowned sculptor Alexander Calder, also majored in engineering.

Rachel Carson, founder of the modern environmental movement and author of *Silent Spring*—the book that led eventually to the creation of the Environmental Protection Agency and the Clean Air and Water acts—graduated from Chatham College with a degree in biology. Best-selling author and Nobel Prize winner Toni Morrison received her degree in English from Howard University in Washington, DC. Pulitzer prize–winning author and columnist Dave Barry received his English degree from Haverford College. Stanford graduate Sally Ride, the first American woman to fly into outer space, majored in physics as well as English.

Like many other confused undergraduates, Federal Reserve Chairman Alan Greenspan switched majors, first enrolling in Julliard to study music but then transferring to New York University where he received a degree in economics. Also an economics major, Donald Trump earned his degree from the Wharton School at the University of Pennsylvania.

Suze Orman, financial guru and self-help author, received her degree in social work from the University of Illinois at Champaign-Urbana. Author Stephen King received his English degree from the University of Maine.

Multiple-award-winning journalist Connie Chung received her bachelor's degree in journalism from the University of Maryland. Comedian Dennis Miller gradated from Point Park College with a journalism degree. Television journalist Jane Pauley graduated from Indiana University, where she majored in political science. Dan Rather graduated in 1953 with a degree in journalism from Sam Houston State Teachers College.

Actress Brooke Shields graduated from Princeton University with a degree in French literature. Famous TV personality Regis Philbin earned a sociology degree at the University of Notre Dame. Steve Martin was a philosophy major at California State University—Long Beach. Denzel Washington received his degree in journalism from Fordham University.

The Reverend Jesse Jackson received a degree in sociology from North Carolina Agricultural and Technical College in Greensboro.

Author Stephen Coonts received a political science degree from West Virginia University. Actor Don Knotts (*Pleasantville*) graduated from the same school with a degree in communication studies.

The University of Cincinnati has numerous celebrity graduates: Joseph Strauss, designer of the Golden Gate Bridge, who majored in engineering; architect Michael Graves, who majored in architecture; George Rieveschl, inventor of antihistamines, majored in chemistry; George Sperti, inventor of Preparation H and frozen orange juice concentrate, majored in engineering.

Actress Edie Falco studied acting at Purchase College—State University of New York, as did Wesley Snipes and Stanley Tucci. Actress Natalie Portman majored in psychology at Harvard University. Jennifer Garner switched from chemistry to a theater major at Denison University.

The Reverend Martin Luther King, Jr., entered Morehouse College at age 15 and in 1948 graduated with his bachelor's degree in sociology. Director Spike Lee also graduated from Morehouse College; he majored in mass communications.

Miami Heat Center Alonzo Mourning also majored in sociology, receiving his degree from Georgetown University. Basketball legend Michael Jordan graduated from the University of North Carolina with a degree in geography in 1986.

Kurt Warner of the St. Louis Rams received his bachelor's degree in public relations in 1994 from the University of Northern Iowa. Former Denver Broncos quarterback John Elway majored in economics at Stanford University.

Before becoming the Indianapolis Colts' quarterback and NFL Most Valuable Player for 2003 and 2004, Peyton Manning played college football at the University of Tennessee. His academic record is nearly as outstanding as his athletic record: he graduated with honors and a 3.6 GPA, and he received his BA in speech communication over the course of only three years

Musician Chris Isaak was an English major at the University of the Pacific in Stockton, California. He has said he fell into music because he couldn't make it right away as a writer. Actress Janet Leigh majored in music therapy at University of the Pacific. Jazz legend Dave Brubeck, another University of the Pacific alumnus, switched from preveterinary medicine to music after the biology department reportedly told him to major in what he really cared about.

Novelist E. L. Doctorow graduated from Kenyon College with a degree in philosophy in 1952. Fellow alumnus Bill Watterson, cartoonist (Calvin and Hobbes), received a degree in political science in 1980 from Kenyon. Chemist Carl Djerassi, inventor of the birth-control pill, received his degree in chemistry from Kenyon in 1943.

Several musicians, including Melissa Etheridge, Steve Smith, Branford Marsalis, and Kevin Eubanks were music majors at Berklee College of Music in Boston, the largest college of music in the world.

Carnegie Mellon's College of Fine Arts has several famous alumni. Stephen Bochco, producer of TV hits *Hill Street Blues, L.A. Law, Murder One,* and *NYPD Blue* majored in theater there, as did John Wells (*ER*), Oscar winner Holly Hunter, Ted Danson (*Cheers, Becker*), Jack Klugman (*The Odd Couple*), Blair Underwood (*L.A. Law*), Albert Brooks (*Broadcast News*), Rene Auberjonois (*Star Trek, The Next Generation*), and Ming-Na Wen (*The Single Guy, ER, The Joy Luck Club*).

Actor George Wendt, who played Norm on *Cheers,* earned his degree in economics from Rockhurst College in Kansas City, Missouri.

Julia Louis-Dreyfus, the irrepressible Elaine on *Seinfeld,* earned a BS degree in speech from Northwestern University in 1982; novelist Saul Bellow earned a BS in sociology in 1937; Richard Gephart of the U.S. Congress received a BS in speech in 1962; and Judge Kenesaw Mountain Landis, the first commissioner of baseball, graduated from Northwestern's School of Law in 1891 when a law degree required only two years of study after high school.

APPENDIX
National
Associations

A number of national organizations provide information and materials to students interested in particular fields. Some of these national associations, with Internet address when available, are listed here. Visit their Web sites, call, or write for information on fields that are of interest to you. Can't decide? Write to all of them! You may find an area of interest in the association material.

Accounting
American Accounting Association
5717 Bessie Drive
Sarasota, FL 34233-2399
(941) 921-7747
aaahq.org/index.cfm

Anthropology
American Anthropological Association
2200 Wilson Boulevard, Suite 600
Arlington, VA 22201
(703) 528-1902
www.aaanet.org

Architecture
American Institute of Architects
1735 New York Avenue NW
Washington, DC 20006
(202) 626-7300
www.aia.org

Art
American Artists Professional League
47 Fifth Avenue
New York, NY 10003
(212) 645-1345
www.americanartistsprofessionalleague.org

National Association of Independent Artists
www.naia-artists.org

Banking
American Bankers Association
1120 Connecticut Avenue NW
Washington, DC 20036
1-800-BANKERS
www.aba.com

Biology
American Institute of Biological Sciences
1444 I Street NW, Suite 200
Washington, DC 20005
(202) 628-1500
www.aibs.org

Brokering
New York Stock Exchange
11 Wall Street
New York, NY 10005
(212) 656-3000
www.nyse.com

National Association of Stock Brokers
5755 Oberlin Drive, Suite 311
San Diego, CA 92121
(800) 222-8627
www.nastockbrokers.com

Chemistry
American Chemical Society
1155 Sixteenth Street NW
Washington, DC 20036
800-227-5558
www.chemistry.org

Civil Engineering
American Society of Civil Engineers
1801 Alexander Bell Drive
Reston, VA 20191-4400
(800) 548-2723
www.asce.org

Communications
National Communication Association
1765 N Street NW
Washington, DC 20036
(202) 464-4622
www.natcom.org

Computer Programming
Association for Computing Machinery
1515 Broadway
New York, NY 10036-5701
(800)-342-6626
www.acm.org

Criminology
National Criminal Justice Association
720 Seventh Street NW, Third Floor
Washington, DC 20001-3716
202-628-8550
www.ncja.org

Dietetics
American Dietetic Association
1120 Connecticut Avenue NW, Suite 480
Washington, DC 20036
(800) 877-0877
www.eatright.ogr

Economics
American Economic Association
2014 Broadway, Suite 305
Nashville, TN 37203-2418
(615) 322-2595
www.vanderbuilt.edu/AEA

Education
National Education Association
1201 Sixteenth Street NW
Washington, DC 20036-3290
(202) 833-4000
www.nea.org

Engineering
National Society of Professional Engineers
1420 King Street
Alexandria, VA 22314-2794
(703) 684-2800
www.nspe.org

Geography
American Geographical Society
120 Wall Street, Suite 100
New York, NY 10005-3904
(212) 422-5456
www.amergeog.org

Geology
American Geological Institute
4220 King Street
Alexandria, VA 22302-1502
(703) 379-2480
www.agiweb.org

History
American Historical Association
400 A Street SE
Washington, DC 20003-3889
(202) 544-2422
www.historians.org

Journalism
American Society of Journalists and Authors
1501 Broadway, Suite 302
New York, NY 10036
(212) 997-0947
www.asja.org

Language Specialist
American Association of Language Specialists
P.O. Box 39339
Washington, DC 20016
(301) 986-1542
www.taals.net

Law
American Bar Association
321 North Clark Street
Chicago, IL 60610
(312) 988-5000
www.abanet.org

Management
American Management Association
1601 Broadway
New York, NY 10019
 (212) 586-8100
www.amanet.org

Marketing
American Marketing Association
311 South Wacker Drive, Suite 5800
Chicago, IL 60606
(800) AMA-1150
www.marketingpower.com

Mathematics
American Mathematical Society
201 Charles Street
Providence, RI 02904-2294
(800) 321-4AMS
www.ams.org

Medicine
Council on Medical Education
American Medical Association
515 N. State Street
Chicago, IL 60610
(800) 621-8335

Music
National Association of Schools of Music
11250 Roger Bacon Drive, Suite 21
Reston, VA 20190-5248
(703) 437-0700
www.nasm.arts-accredit.org

Oceanography
National Association of Marine Surveyors
P.O. Box 9306
Chesapeake, VA 23321-9306
(800) 822-6267
www.nams-cms.org

Pharmaceuticals
American Pharmaceutical Association
2215 Constitution Avenue NW
Washington, DC 20037-2985
(800) 237-APhA
www.aphanet.org

Philosophy
American Philosophical Society
104 S. Fifth Street
Philadelphia, PA 19106-3387
(215) 440-3400
www.amphilsoc.org

Political Science
American Political Science Association
1527 New Hampshire Avenue NW
Washington, DC 20036-1206
(202) 483-2512
www.apsanet.org

Psychologist
American Psychological Association
750 First Street NE
Washington, DC 20002-4242
(800) 374-2721
www.apa.org

Public Relations
The Public Relations Society of America
33 Maiden Lane, 11th Floor
New York, NY 10038-5150
212-460-1400
www.prsa.org

Sociology
American Sociological Association
1307 New York Avenue NW, Suite 700
Washington, DC 20005
(202) 383-9005
www.asanet.org

Theater
American Alliance for Theatre and Education
7475 Wisconsin Avenue, Suite 300A
Bethesda, MD 20814
(301) 951-7977
www.aate.com

Writing
National Writer's Association
10940 S. Parker Road, #508
Parker, CO 80134
303-841-0246
www.nationalwriters.com